Anxious Attachment Detox

Uncover Toxic Patterns to Let Go of Abandonment Fears, Manage Insecurities, and Regain Your Confidence to Build Healthy Relationships - From Clingy to Secure in Love

A.J BROOKS

Copyright © 2024 by A.J BROOKS

All rights reserved.

No portion of this book may be reproduced in any form without written permission from the publisher or author, except as permitted by U.S. copyright law. This publication is designed to provide accurate and authoritative information in regard to the subject matter covered.

It is sold with the understanding that neither the author nor the publisher is engaged in rendering legal, investment, accounting or other professional services.

While the publisher and author have used their best efforts in preparing this book, they make no representations or warranties with respect to the accuracy or completeness of the contents of this book and specifically disclaim any implied warranties of merchantability or fitness for a particular purpose.

No warranty may be created or extended by sales representatives or written sales materials. The advice and strategies contained herein may not be suitable for your situation.

You should consult with a professional when appropriate. Neither the publisher nor the author shall be liable for any loss of profit or any other commercial damages, including but not limited to special, incidental, consequential, personal, or other damages.

Contents

Introduction	vii
1. FOUNDATIONS OF ANXIOUS ATTACHMENT	1
The Science Behind Anxious Attachment: Decoding Your Bonds	1
Historical Roots: How Past Relationships Shape Your Present	4
Recognizing Anxious Behaviors in Daily Interactions	6
The Spectrum of Attachment: Where Do You Fall?	9
Self-Assessment: Identifying Your Attachment Style	11
2. IDENTIFYING TOXIC PATTERNS	15
The Cycle of Neediness and Rejection	15
Overcoming the Urge to Overanalyze Partner's Actions	18
The Jealousy Trap: Navigating Through Insecurities	21
The Fear of Abandonment: Breaking Down the Walls	24
The Cycle of Push and Pull in Relationships	27
People-Pleasing: When the Desire to be Liked Overwhelms	29
3. BUILDING SELF-ESTEEM AND INDEPENDENCE	33
Cultivating Self-Worth: Exercises and Strategies	33
Embracing Solitude: Finding Strength in Being Alone	36
Developing a Secure Sense of Self	39
The Fear of Missing Out in Relationships	41
From Self-Criticism to Self-Compassion	43
4. EMOTIONAL REGULATION AND MINDFULNESS	47
Mindfulness Practices for Relationship Anxiety	47
Identifying Triggers: A Guide to Emotional Awareness	50
Self-Soothing Techniques for Immediate Relief	52

    Cultivating Emotional Resilience   56
    Breaking Free from the Overthinking Loop   58

5. EFFECTIVE COMMUNICATION STRATEGIES   61
    Assertive Communication: Expressing Your Needs   61
    Listening Skills: The Key to Understanding   64
    Navigating Difficult Conversations with Grace   67
    Feedback vs. Criticism: How to Tell the Difference   70
    Resolving Conflicts without Losing Yourself   73

6. HEALTHY DATING PRACTICES FOR THE ANXIOUSLY ATTACHED   77
    Navigating Dating Apps Without Anxiety   77
    The Dos and Don'ts of Early Dating Stages   80
    Recognizing Red Flags and Deal Breakers   83
    Setting Healthy Pace and Boundaries in New Relationships   85
    The Importance of Maintaining Individuality in Early Dating   87

7. LONG-TERM RELATIONSHIP SUCCESS   91
    Keeping Love Alive: Relationship Nurturing Techniques   91
    Balancing Togetherness and Independence   93
    Effective Coping Strategies for Relationship Anxiety   97
    The Role of Shared Goals and Values in Long-term Stability   99
    Renewing Commitment: When Relationships Hit Rough Patches   102

8. FOSTERING HEALTHY RELATIONSHIP DYNAMICS   105
    The Art of Giving and Receiving in Love   105
    Detoxing from Codependency: Steps to Independence   108
    Recognizing and Choosing Emotionally Available Partners   110
    Dealing with Ghosting and Uncertainty in Dating   112
    Breakup Recovery: Moving Forward with Grace and Strength   115
    When to Hold On and When to Let Go   117

9. TOOLS FOR EVERYDAY ANXIETIES ... 121
   Managing Anxiety in High-Stress Situations ... 121
   Journaling for Self-Discovery and Healing ... 124
   The Role of Physical Activity in Anxiety Reduction ... 126
   Nutrition and Mental Health: What You Need to Know ... 128
   Rewiring Your Brain: Techniques for Positive Thinking ... 130

10. SHADOW WORK AND ANXIOUS ATTACHMENT ... 135
    Introduction to Shadow Work: Healing Hidden Wounds ... 135
    Identifying Your Shadow: Exercises for Self-Discovery ... 137
    Shadow Work Techniques for Releasing Old Patterns ... 139
    Integrating the Shadow: Towards Wholeness and Healing ... 141
    Shadow Work and Relationships: Healing Together ... 143

11. EMBRACING A SECURE FUTURE ... 147
    The Journey from Anxious to Secure Attachment ... 147
    Cultivating Self-Love: Beyond the Buzzword ... 149
    The Role of Forgiveness in Healing Attachment Wounds ... 152
    Preparing for Setbacks: Resilience in the Healing Process ... 153
    Secure Attachment in Action: Success Stories ... 155

    Conclusion ... 159
    References ... 163

Introduction

Have you ever caught yourself staring at your phone, hoping for a message that never arrives? Maybe you've had nights replaying conversations in your mind, deciphering every word and gesture for hints of fading affection. You may carry a worry deep inside that those you hold dear may one day walk away despite reassurances of their love. If these scenarios seem too familiar, you're likely experiencing what experts call anxious attachment. This isn't just a passing concern; it's a fear of abandonment that can overshadow your entire existence, turning love into a hazardous journey rather than a source of solace.

You're not the one grappling with this. Anxious attachment can create feelings of solitude, making it seem like everyone else effortlessly navigates relationships while you are struggling. This book aims to validate your emotions and, importantly, guide you towards overcoming fear and finding security—a transformation from heartache to healing.

This book is designed to help you shift from an attachment style filled with apprehension to a secure attachment style defined by confidence and peace in your relationships.

Everyone seeks stability in relationships, but if you have an anxious attachment style, this may feel like an uphill battle. This journey through these pages aims to help you understand why you feel the way you do, how these patterns developed, and most importantly, how to break free from them.

Throughout this exploration, we will delve into a mix of attachment theory, practical recovery techniques, and valuable self-help resources such as shadow work journaling prompts and self-assessment quizzes. This unique blend sets this book apart from others. Whether you've been disappointed by efforts to change your relationship dynamics or are just starting to grasp the reasons behind your romantic interactions, here, you'll discover new perspectives and actionable solutions.

Drawing from years of research and conquering my own anxious attachments, I've infused all my experiences and professional knowledge into ensuring that this book not only explains what's happening but also empowers you to make tangible changes. I recognize the bravery needed to confront these seated fears. My aim is to support you through every stage of reclaiming your independence and fostering healthier connections.

It's totally normal to have doubts, especially if you've attempted to adjust these patterns in the past without success. Rest assured, the techniques and insights shared here are based on established psychological principles and enriched by personal victories over similar challenges. This isn't just theory; it's an approach, a set of resources designed to help you flourish in both love and life.

So, I encourage you to embrace this with a heart and a sharp mind. Dive into the exercises wholeheartedly, ponder deeply the stories and data provided, and begin to perceive yourself from a perspective. Change is not just achievable; it's within your reach.

Let this book mark the beginning of your journey towards a future where relationships no longer cause anxiety but become pillars of strength and happiness. Together, let's progress towards a style that fosters security where love isn't about mere survival but about celebrating connections.

Chapter 1

Foundations of Anxious Attachment

Have you ever wondered why certain relationships, no matter how promising they begin, end up feeling like you're navigating a storm without a compass? Perhaps it's the pang in your chest when a text goes unanswered, or the way your heart sinks when plans change unexpectedly, triggering a whirlwind of worry and doubt. These sensations aren't just fleeting moments of insecurity; they are signals from deep within your attachment system, a complex emotional landscape sculpted by your earliest experiences and relationships. This chapter is dedicated to unraveling the mysteries of anxious attachment. It aims to offer you not just understanding, but a transformative insight that can lead to profound emotional liberation and healthier relationships.

The Science Behind Anxious Attachment: Decoding Your Bonds

Biological Basis

Our journey into understanding anxious attachment begins with a look into our very biology. Human beings are wired for connection — our survival has historically depended on it. From the moment we enter the world, our brain begins to form pathways that will influence how we connect with other people throughout our lives. Neurochemicals like oxytocin, known as the 'love hormone,' play a pivotal role. In moments of closeness and bonding, oxytocin floods our system, reinforcing the sense of security and attachment. However, for those with an anxious attachment style, this system can become overactivated. In situations where attachment is threatened, the body can produce higher levels of cortisol, a stress hormone, leading to the intense anxiety and fear of abandonment often experienced by individuals with this attachment style.

Attachment Theory Explained

To further understand anxious attachment, we turn to John Bowlby's groundbreaking attachment theory, which has illuminated the importance of early relationships in shaping our attachment styles. According to Bowlby, the interactions you had with your primary caregivers set the blueprint for your future relationships. If caregivers were inconsistently available or unpredictably responsive, you might develop an anxious attachment style characterized by a chronic fear of abandonment and an acute sensitivity to relational cues. In adulthood, this can translate into behaviors such as clinging or seeking constant reassurance from partners.

Modern Psychological Perspectives

Building on Bowlby's foundational theory, modern psychology introduces nuances that help explain how anxious attachment evolves over time. Erik Erikson's stages of psychosocial development, for instance, show us how trust established in early infancy impacts later stages, such as identity formation in adolescence and intimacy in young adulthood. Anxiously attached individuals might struggle particularly with Erikson's stage of intimacy versus isolation, wrestling with vulnerability and trust. Contemporary research also explores how our attachment systems can be reshaped and healed through meaningful relationships and therapeutic interventions, offering hope to those who wish to shift towards more secure attachment patterns.

Impact on Adult Relationships

Understanding the science of attachment is crucial because it directly affects the dynamics of your adult relationships. Recognizing that your fears and behaviors have a biological and psychological foundation can be liberating. It allows you to see that your feelings of insecurity or need for reassurance are not flaws but signals of underlying processes shaped by early experiences and reinforced by biological responses. This knowledge empowers you to approach your attachment fears with compassion rather than judgment.

Securing Adult Attachments

The quest for secure adult attachments is both challenging and rewarding. It involves recognizing the patterns that govern your relationships and consciously moving towards behaviors that foster security and trust. For adults with an anxious attachment style, this might include learning to self-soothe, developing healthier communication habits, and gradually recalibrating their attachment expectations. The correlation between anxious attachment and relationship satisfaction is clear: the more secure you feel within yourself, the more satisfying and stable your relationships will become.

Attachment Styles and Personality

Finally, it's essential to acknowledge the profound impact that your attachment style has on your personality. Traits like sensitivity to rejection or heightened emotional responsiveness often seen in those with anxious attachment can be understood as adaptations to early relational environments. While these traits may have been protective once, in adulthood, they can complicate relationships. Recognizing this can help you appreciate your full personality spectrum and foster characteristics that lead to healthier interactions and a more secure attachment style.

Understanding the foundations of anxious attachment is the first step toward transformation. Armed with this knowledge, you are better prepared to tackle the specific challenges posed by this attachment style, paving the way for richer, more fulfilling relationships. As we move forward, remember that each piece of information is a tool in your hands, crafted to help you sculpt a more secure, confident self.

Historical Roots: How Past Relationships Shape Your Present

Understanding the early interactions with caregivers can be akin to peering through a window into the formation of our current relational dynamics. For those grappling with anxious attachment, these initial relationships often set a pattern of expectation and response that extends far into adulthood. The role of caregivers in our early life does more than just provide us with immediate comfort or distress; it fundamentally shapes our outlook on how secure or precarious relationships can be. For instance, consider a child whose cries are met inconsistently—sometimes with soothing warmth, other times with neglect or irritation. Such experiences can engrain a deep-seated sense of uncertainty and a subconscious belief that love and attention are conditional and unpredictable.

This inconsistency can lead to what we often term as 'anxious attachment.' As adults, individuals might find themselves replicating similar dynamics experienced in childhood, perhaps unconsciously seeking partners who echo the familiarity of earlier relational patterns, despite how tumultuous or unfulfilling those relationships might be. This replication isn't about comfort in the traditional sense but rather a deep-rooted compulsion to recreate and, hopefully, resolve unfinished emotional business from childhood.

Furthermore, the echo of past traumas plays a significant role. Traumas such as neglect, emotional unavailability of caregivers, or even more overt forms of abuse can distort one's perception of self-worth and skew the lens through which one views relational stability. Unresolved, these traumas linger, manifesting as fears of abandonment or an overwhelming need for closeness that might overwhelm partners who do not understand the source of these intense emotions. Recognizing these patterns can often feel like unearthing layers of deeply buried truths about ourselves and our histories, yet it is a critical step towards healing.

The environment in which one grows up also significantly impacts attachment styles. Factors like the overall emotional climate of the home, the nature of the parents' relationship with each other, cultural attitudes towards relationships and autonomy, and even broader societal influences shape how one learns to connect with others. For example, in a family where emotions are rarely discussed openly, a child might grow up feeling that their emotional needs are unimportant, learning to suppress their feelings and, by extension, their needs for emotional closeness, thereby fostering an anxious attachment style.

As one transitions from childhood into adulthood, these early attachment experiences often become predictors of how one will interact in adult romantic relationships. The patterns set by early attachments influence how one navigates closeness and distance, dependency, and autonomy. For those with an anxious attachment style, the move towards adult relationships might be marked by a search for the security and consistency they lacked in earlier life stages. This search, however, can sometimes lead to relationships that cyclically replicate past dynamics rather than correcting them.

Implicit and explicit memories of these early experiences also play a crucial role. While we may not consciously remember every interaction with our caregivers, our implicit memory stores away the emotional residues of these interactions. These memories, though not always accessible through direct recall, influence our expectations and reactions in our current relationships. The way a person's body tenses up when they feel ignored, or the inexplicable anxiety triggered by a partner's casual remark can often be traced back to these implicit memories.

Lastly, breaking the cycle of anxious attachment, particularly when it has been passed down through generations, requires both awareness and intentional action. It involves recognizing the patterns, understanding their roots, and consciously choosing different behaviors and responses. It's about creating new experiences in relationships that can rewrite old narratives, fostering a sense of security that might have been missing before. This process is neither quick nor easy, but it is possible, and it starts with understanding the profound impact our past relationships have on our present and future selves.

Recognizing Anxious Behaviors in Daily Interactions

In the tapestry of daily life, certain threads pull tighter than others, shaping how we respond to the world around us. For those with an anxious attachment style, these threads can often lead to a pattern of behaviors that, while initially serving as emotional safeguards, may eventually weave a fabric of distress and misunderstanding in relationships. Recognizing these behaviors as they unfold in day-to-day interactions can be transformative, allowing for a recalibration of responses and fostering healthier relational dynamics.

Identifying Triggers

The first step in this recalibration process involves identifying what specific situations trigger anxious behaviors. Common triggers might include delays in communication, such as a postponed text or an unanswered call, which can set off internal alarms for someone with anxious attachment. Changes in a partner's routine or tone of voice might also act as triggers, interpreted as signs of waning interest or affection. Even social events that require sharing a partner's attention can become a source of stress, stirring up fears of displacement or neglect. Recognizing these triggers is akin to mapping the landscapes of your emotional world; it helps you understand where your feelings of insecurity intensify and why they might do so.

Anxious Behaviors Unpacked

Once triggers are identified, the next layer of understanding involves unpacking the behaviors these triggers elicit. Individuals with anxious attachment might find themselves seeking constant reassurance from their partners to quell the insecurity that these triggers provoke. This reassurance is often sought through frequent texts or calls, a need for repeated affirmations of love and commitment, or a constant desire for physical proximity. Overthinking is another expected behavior, where normal interactions are dissected for hidden meanings, leading to a cascade of interpretations often rooted more in fear than in reality. Trust issues may also surface, not necessarily from any deceit or wrongdoing by partners but from a deep-seated fear that they will inevitably leave or become disinterested. These behaviors, while understandable, can strain relationships, creating cycles of dependency and frustration.

The Role of Communication

How individuals communicate in relationships is profoundly affected by their attachment style. For those with anxious attachment, there can be a tendency towards passive communication, where instead of directly stating needs or concerns, there is a reliance on hints or indirect signals, hoping the partner will intuitively understand. This indirectness can stem from a fear of confrontation or rejection, believing that if they state their needs directly, it may drive the partner away. However, this style of communication often leads to misunderstandings and unmet expectations, fueling further anxiety. Conversely, during moments of heightened insecurity, communication might swing to the opposite extreme of confrontational or accusatory, especially if the anxious individual feels ignored or sidelined. These communication swings— from passive to aggressive—can confuse partners and escalate conflicts, undermining the sense of security and understanding in the relationship.

Self-Monitoring Techniques

Addressing these patterns begins with self-monitoring, a technique that involves observing and noting one's own behaviors and emotional responses as they occur. This practice does not involve judgment or immediate attempts to change but instead encourages a stance of curious observation. By keeping a daily log of when you feel most anxious in your relationship, what seems to trigger it, and how you respond, patterns begin to emerge. This log can include notes on what was happening immediately before you felt anxious, the thoughts that went through your mind, and how you reacted— whether by reaching out to your partner, withdrawing, or perhaps starting an argument. Over time, this log will help not only identify the most common triggers and your typical responses but also recognize the effectiveness of your reactions. Did seeking reassurance actually alleviate your anxiety, or did it lead to a cycle of repeated reassurances? Did your partner respond positively to indirect hints, or did it result in confusion? This self-awareness is crucial in beginning to change these ingrained patterns, setting a foundation for more secure and resilient ways of relating to those you love.

The Spectrum of Attachment: Where Do You Fall?

Understanding the concept of the attachment spectrum is akin to recognizing that human emotions and relationships are not black and white, but rather a gradient of complex hues. It is essential to grasp that attachment styles exist along a continuum, providing a more fluid and nuanced view of how we relate to others. This perspective helps us appreciate that these styles are not fixed life sentences but dynamic states that can evolve with self-awareness and effort.

At one end of this spectrum lies secure attachment, where individuals feel comfortable with intimacy and autonomy. They are also capable of maintaining healthy and long-term relationships. On the other end, we find avoidant and anxious attachment styles, where individuals might struggle with intimacy and dependence in various ways. If you find yourself overreacting to relational cues, needing frequent reassurance, or perhaps feeling unworthy of love unless you are constantly validated, you might lean towards the anxious side of this spectrum. These reactions are not random but are deeply ingrained responses that can be traced back to your earliest experiences with caregivers and significant others.

The characteristics of anxious attachment are profound and often painful. You might recognize in yourself a hypersensitivity to your partner's moods and behaviors, reading deeply into offhand remarks or normal shifts in communication. This might lead to a perpetual state of emotional tumult, where calmness seems ever elusive. You may also notice a pattern of clinging to relationships, driven by a fear that being alone equates to being unloved or abandoned. In contrast, those with avoidant attachment might seem distant, self-sufficient to a fault, often pulling away at the first sign of real closeness.

Comparing these styles, it becomes evident that each has its distinct challenges and tendencies. While the securely attached enjoy stable and fulfilling relationships, those with anxious attachment wrestle with insecurity and constant worry about their relationships' stability. Avoidantly attached individuals, meanwhile, might avoid deep relationships altogether, perceiving them as threatening their independence. These styles are not merely labels but reflect deep-seated beliefs about oneself and the nature of love and trust.

Most importantly, the attachment styles are fluid rather than fixed. This fluidity is a beacon of hope for anyone who recognizes the pain and limitations of an anxious attachment style. With intentional efforts, such as engaging in therapy, pursuing personal growth opportunities, or making conscious relationship choices, it is entirely possible to move closer to a secure attachment style. This shift does not occur overnight and requires patience and persistence. It involves gradually rewriting the internal narratives about self-worth and relational security and actively practicing new ways of relating to others.

Imagine, for a moment, the possibility of reacting to a missed call with a sense of calm rather than a cascade of anxiety, or expressing your needs without the overwhelming fear of driving someone away. These are the fruits of moving towards a more secure attachment style, and they are within your reach. Each step towards understanding and reshaping your attachment style is a step towards more enriching and less fear-driven relationships. It is about breaking free from the invisible chains that bind you to old patterns and stepping into a space where love is experienced as a source of joy rather than anxiety.

As we continue exploring these concepts, remember that understanding is the first step towards change. By identifying where you currently fall on the attachment spectrum, you can begin to navigate toward a style of relating that brings not just security but profound satisfaction and resilience to your relationships. This understanding allows you to approach your interactions with clarity and compassion, both for yourself and for others, paving the way for deeper connections and a more fulfilling love life.

Self-Assessment: Identifying Your Attachment Style

Self-awareness is a powerful first step in transforming the way you experience love and relationships. It is akin to turning on a light in a room that has been dim for too long, revealing corners and spaces that were once hidden in shadows. This process begins with a clear understanding of your own attachment style, which serves as a map to guide your path to secure attachment. Here, we will explore various validated self-assessment tools and reflective exercises designed to help you identify your attachment style accurately and understand its profound impact on your relationships.

One of the most effective tools for identifying your attachment style is the Adult Attachment Interview (AAI). This structured interview helps you reflect on your childhood experiences and the impact they have on your behavior in relationships as an adult. By discussing your past with a trained professional, patterns often emerge that highlight your attachment style—whether secure, anxious, or avoidant. Additionally, self-report questionnaires like the Experiences in Close Relationships-Revised (ECR-R) questionnaire provide a more accessible yet equally revealing look into your attachment tendencies. These questionnaires typically ask about your feelings and behaviors in close relationships, helping to pinpoint how often you experience anxiety or avoidance in relation to others.

Reflecting on your past relationships can also be incredibly enlightening. As you look back, consider the recurring themes and issues. Did you often feel worried about your partner's commitment or affection? Did you find yourself needing frequent reassurance of their feelings towards you? Perhaps you noticed a pattern of overwhelming fear that your loved ones might leave you, even when there was no real indication of trouble. These reflections are not about casting judgment on yourself or your past partners but about understanding the recurring patterns that signify an anxious attachment style.

Understanding how your attachment style influences your needs and behavior in relationships is another crucial aspect of this self-assessment. If you have an anxious attachment style, you might notice that you have a deep-seated need for closeness and security, which can sometimes manifest as clinginess or dependency. Recognizing these needs isn't about feeling flawed; it's about gaining clarity on what drives your behaviors so you can address them constructively. For instance, understanding that your need for constant reassurance stems from attachment anxieties allows you to communicate these needs to your partner more effectively, rather than feeling ashamed or acting out.

Positioning self-assessment as the first step towards change is vital. It equips you with the knowledge and insights needed to begin reshaping your attachment style. This is not about overhauling who you are but about adjusting the learned behaviors and emotional responses that no longer serve you well. It's about replacing fear and insecurity with confidence and trust, both in yourself and in your relationships.

The good news is that attachment styles are not static; they can change over time with self-awareness and intentional action. Psychological interventions, particularly those focused on developing secure attachment patterns, such as Cognitive Behavioral Therapy (CBT) or Attachment-Based Therapy, can be highly effective. These therapies work by helping you understand and reframe your attachment-related thoughts and behaviors, gradually guiding you toward a more secure way of relating to others. Additionally, everyday practices such as mindfulness meditation and communication skills training can empower you to manage anxiety and build healthier, more secure relationships.

As you engage with these self-assessment tools and reflect on your relationship patterns, remember that this process is about growth and healing. It's about taking what you learn about yourself and using it to forge more profound, more satisfying connections with those you love. Each insight you gain is a step forward, not just toward securing healthier relationships but also toward embracing a fuller, more balanced sense of self. In this light, self-assessment is not just a tool for relationship improvement; it's a gateway to personal transformation.

Chapter 2

Identifying Toxic Patterns

In the dance of relationships, certain steps can lead us repeatedly into the arms of distress and dissatisfaction. Recognizing these patterns is crucial, not because it offers an immediate solution, but because it provides the map from which we can begin charting a new course. This chapter focuses on one such pervasive pattern often experienced by those with an anxious attachment style—the cycle of neediness and rejection. Here, you'll learn to identify and understand this cycle, recognize the underlying fears that fuel it, and discover practical strategies for cultivating more secure and satisfying connections.

The Cycle of Neediness and Rejection

At the heart of anxious attachment lies a paradox: the very behaviors adopted to secure a relationship can often push a partner away, initiating a painful cycle of neediness and rejection. Imagine this: you feel an overwhelming need for closeness and reassurance from your partner, so much so that it leads you to seek constant contact or affirmation of their feelings for you. While this is driven by a desire to feel loved and secure, it can be perceived by your partner as smothering or overly dependent, which might lead them to withdraw. This withdrawal then validates your original fear of abandonment, increasing your anxiety and neediness—a cycle that can be as exhausting as it is heart-wrenching.

Understanding the Cycle

To truly understand this cycle, it's essential to recognize that the need for reassurance isn't inherently problematic. It becomes toxic only when it stems from deep-seated insecurities and fears of rejection that are so intense that they lead to behaviors that suffocate the very relationship you wish to preserve. These behaviors often include excessive calling or texting, needing to be constantly with your partner, or requiring frequent verbal reassurances of their commitment.

Fear of Rejection

The engine driving this cycle is a profound fear of rejection. This fear isn't just about being left; it's intertwined with a deeper fear of not being worthy of love unless you are constantly validated by someone else. It's a fear that whispers you might not be good enough, that without your partner, your value diminishes. This fear can be so pervasive that it colors every interaction with your partner, turning what might be ordinary moments into tests of commitment and affection.

Breaking the Cycle

Breaking free from this cycle begins with self-awareness. It's about recognizing the moments when you're acting out of fear rather than genuine connection. Are you texting your partner repeatedly because you miss them or because you're scared they're losing interest? Pausing to ask yourself these questions can be the first step in interrupting the cycle. Another powerful strategy is developing what psychologists call 'differentiation'—the ability to maintain your sense of self, even in close relationships. This means finding fulfillment and self-assurance not just from your relationships but from your own life and passions. When your well-being doesn't solely hinge on your partner's presence or moods, the grip of neediness begins to loosen.

Building Secure Connections

Finally, fostering secure connections involves enhancing the quality of communication in your relationships. It's about expressing your needs and fears without letting them dictate your behaviors. This might mean saying to your partner, "I'm feeling insecure right now, and I could use some reassurance," instead of sending a barrage of texts or questions. It involves creating a space where vulnerabilities are shared, not as accusations or demands, but as invitations for deeper understanding and intimacy. Effective communication can transform the cycle of neediness and rejection into a dance of mutual support and assurance.

Reflection Exercise: Identifying Your Patterns

To further aid in breaking this cycle, consider engaging in a simple yet revealing reflection exercise. Take a moment to jot down instances from past relationships where you felt rejected or feared abandonment. Reflect on how you responded to these situations. Did your actions bring you closer to your partner, or did they push them away? Understanding these patterns is the first step toward changing them. This exercise isn't about self-criticism but about recognizing opportunities for growth and healing.

By understanding and addressing the cycle of neediness and rejection, you can begin to cultivate healthier, more secure ways of connecting with those you love. This chapter invites you to step back, examine your relational dance, and learn new steps that lead to a more fulfilling partnership where fears are calmed, needs are met with compassion, and love is secured not through demand but through mutual respect and understanding.

Overcoming the Urge to Overanalyze Partner's Actions

In the intricate dance of relationships, there's a common misstep that many of us who lean towards anxious attachment styles often make: the urge to overanalyze every action, word, or silence from our partners. This habit, usually referred to as 'analysis paralysis,' can feel like an inescapable trap, drawing us deeper into the maze of our insecurities and doubts. It is as if each action of our partner is a piece of a puzzle that we must solve to ensure the security of our relationship. However, this constant scrutiny not only exhausts us but can also strain the very bonds we fear losing.

The Analysis Paralysis

Analysis paralysis in relationships typically manifests as an obsessive need to interpret and predict the meaning behind every minor detail of our partner's behavior. Did they take too long to reply because they are losing interest? Was their tone of voice indicative of annoyance or, worse, indifference? This overinterpretation often stems from an understandable desire to avoid pain and rejection; however, it inadvertently sets a stage where the noise of our anxieties overshadows genuine connection. The impact is profound: it can lead to misunderstandings, create tension, and foster a climate of mistrust and constant uncertainty in the relationship.

Cognitive Distortions

Driving this overanalysis are often cognitive distortions—those tricky, automatic thoughts that distort reality, making situations seem far worse or different than they actually are. Common distortions include 'mind reading' (assuming you know what your partner is thinking), 'catastrophizing' (imagining the worst possible outcome in every situation), and 'personalization' (believing that everything others do is some kind of direct, personal reaction to you). These distorted patterns of thinking fuel the cycle of overanalysis, as every action of your partner is filtered through a lens of skewed perceptions and unfounded assumptions.

To tackle these distortions, it's crucial to recognize them first. This recognition can be an enlightening moment, a break in the clouds allowing you to see how these patterns have been coloring your interpretation of your partner's actions. Awareness alone can be profoundly liberating, reducing the urge to spiral into overanalysis every time a doubt creeps in.

Mindfulness-Based Strategies

One of the most effective tools to combat the habit of overanalyzing is mindfulness. This practice involves staying present and fully engaged in the moment without judgment. By nurturing mindfulness, you can learn to observe your thoughts and feelings about your partner's actions without immediately reacting to them. For instance, when the urge to dissect a casual comment arises, mindfulness encourages you to notice this impulse, acknowledge it, and then let it pass without engagement. Over time, this practice can help decrease the intensity and frequency of overanalytical thoughts, fostering a sense of calm and clarity in your interactions.

A simple mindfulness exercise to start with involves mindful breathing. Whenever you find yourself slipping into analysis paralysis, pause and take ten deep, focused breaths. Concentrate solely on the sensation of breathing—the cool air flowing into your nostrils and the warm air exiting. This brief pause can disrupt the automaticity of anxious thoughts and provide a moment of reprieve, allowing you to approach the situation more calmly.

Fostering Trust and Security

Ultimately, the antidote to the urge to overanalyze lies in nurturing a foundation of trust and security within your relationship. This process begins with open, honest communication about your fears and insecurities. Expressing your feelings without accusing or demanding can open doors to understanding and mutual support. For instance, instead of saying, "You always ignore my texts," try expressing, "I feel anxious when I don't hear from you, as it makes me feel less connected to you." Such vulnerability can foster intimacy and trust, as it helps your partner to understand your inner world without feeling blamed or controlled.

Additionally, actively deciding to give your partner the benefit of the doubt can be a significant step towards building trust. This doesn't mean ignoring your feelings or tolerating unacceptable behavior, but rather choosing to trust your partner's intentions unless proven otherwise. It's about shifting from a mindset of suspicion to one of trust, where open dialogue can thrive and genuine understanding can be nurtured.

By addressing the habit of overanalyzing through understanding cognitive distortions, practicing mindfulness, and fostering an environment of trust and security, you can gradually reduce the strain this habit places on your relationships. Remember, the goal is not to suppress your concern or ignore potential red flags but to cultivate a balanced perspective that enhances the health and happiness of your relationship.

The Jealousy Trap: Navigating Through Insecurities

In the landscape of love and relationships, jealousy often appears like an uninvited guest, stirring unrest and insecurity. At its core, jealousy is not about love but fear—fear of loss, fear of inadequacy, and fear of not being enough. This emotional response can be intense and consuming, especially for those with a preoccupied attachment style, where the need for assurance and fear of abandonment are already heightened. Understanding the roots of jealousy and learning how to navigate through these insecurities is crucial not only for the health of your relationships but also for your personal well-being.

Roots of Jealousy

Jealousy typically springs from a deep well of insecurity and a fragile sense of self-worth. Suppose you've ever felt a surge of jealousy in your relationship. In that case, it might have been triggered by seeing your partner laughing with someone else, spending time away from you, or even just mentioning someone else with admiration. At that moment, it's easy to feel threatened, as if those interactions somehow diminish your value in your partner's eyes. This feeling often stems from an internal narrative that equates your partner's interest in others with a devaluation of your worth. However, it's crucial to recognize that these feelings are more about your self-perception than about your partner's actions. They are reflections of your fears and insecurities, magnified by the lens of anxious attachment, which often interprets ambiguous situations as threats.

Impact of Jealousy

The effects of jealousy extend beyond momentary discomfort, seeping into and potentially eroding the foundation of trust and openness that relationships thrive on. When jealousy becomes a frequent visitor in your interactions, it can lead to behaviors that push your partner away—constant questioning, accusations, or even snooping. These actions, while driven by a desire to feel secure, ironically foster distance and mistrust between partners. For you, the experience of jealousy is equally painful, often spiraling into cycles of self-doubt, anger, and sadness. It's a turbulent emotional state that not only strains your relationship but also impacts your mental health, leading to increased anxiety and possibly even depression.

Strategies for Managing Jealousy

Managing jealousy involves a combination of self-reflection, communication, and emotional regulation. First, when feelings of jealousy arise, take a moment to pause and reflect on what is driving these feelings. Ask yourself, "What am I really afraid of?" and "Is there actual evidence to support my fears, or am I filling in the blanks with my insecurities?" This introspective approach can help you understand the root of your jealousy and differentiate between perceived and real threats.

A practical technique to manage jealousy is the "grounding technique," which helps redirect your attention from spiraling thoughts to the present moment. This can be as simple as focusing on your breathing, counting backward from 100, or engaging your senses by noting five things you can see, four things you can touch, three things you can hear, two things you can smell, and one thing you can taste. This method not only calms your immediate emotional response but also gives you space to assess the situation more objectively.

Communication also plays an important role in handling jealousy. Expressing your feelings openly and honestly, without accusation or demand, can foster understanding and empathy in your relationship. Instead of saying, "You're always flirting with others," try framing your feelings from your perspective, "I feel insecure when I see you with others, and I need some reassurance." This non-confrontational approach invites your partner to understand your emotional landscape without feeling attacked, making it more likely for them to respond with support and reassurance.

Building Self-Esteem

At its heart, combating jealousy is about building a stronger, more compassionate relationship with yourself. It's about bolstering your self-esteem so that your sense of worth is not reliant on external validation, but rooted deeply in your self-awareness and self-acceptance. Engaging in activities and pursuits that reinforce your sense of identity and accomplishment can significantly boost your self-esteem. Whether it's through creative endeavors, physical activities, or intellectual pursuits, find and nurture passions that make you feel competent and fulfilled independently of your relationship.

Additionally, practicing self-compassion is vital. Be gentle with yourself when feelings of jealousy arise. Recognize that feeling jealous occasionally is part of being human and not a reflection of your inadequacy or worth. Treat yourself with the same kindness and understanding you would offer a good friend in your situation. This compassionate self-relationship can transform how you experience and react to jealousy, shifting from self-criticism to self-support.

By understanding the roots of jealousy, recognizing its impact, employing strategies to manage it, and working on building your self-esteem, you can navigate through these insecurities more effectively. These efforts will not only enhance your relationship dynamics but also lead to a more secure and contented you, where jealousy no longer holds the power to disrupt but becomes a signal to connect more deeply with yourself and your loved ones.

The Fear of Abandonment: Breaking Down the Walls

Understanding the labyrinthine corridors of the human heart, particularly when navigating the fear of abandonment, is akin to exploring a hidden cave where each step echoes memories of past hurts and betrayals. This fear is not merely a fleeting concern but a profound emotional response that can color every aspect of your relationships. It stems from experiences where the essential emotional support needed was unpredictably available or entirely absent, leaving a residue of insecurity that persists into adult relationships. This fear manifests in various ways, from preemptively distancing oneself from partners to avoid potential pain, to clinging too tightly for fear that any moment of separation might become permanent.

The origins of abandonment fear are often traced back to early life experiences. Children who experience loss, inconsistency in caregiving, or emotional neglect can grow into adults who expect that others will not be reliable or that relationships will inevitably end in pain. These experiences teach them that to love is to risk abandonment, embedding a trigger in their emotional blueprint that activates whenever closeness threatens to become closeness lost. It's a protective mechanism, deeply ingrained, yet one that ironically often leads to the very abandonment it seeks to prevent.

For those who live with this fear, understanding its triggers is crucial. It might be a partner's casual comment about needing space, a missed call, or even a change in routine that can spiral into anxiety and panic. Recognizing these triggers does more than provide insight—it is the first step in reclaiming control over your emotional responses. This awareness lets you anticipate and prepare rather than react and regret. It helps you to distinguish between present reality and the shadows of past fears that might be coloring your perception.

Self-Soothing Techniques

Navigating through the stormy emotions that abandonment fears can stir requires effective self-soothing techniques. These techniques are vital tools that allow you to manage your emotional responses and maintain equilibrium during moments of perceived threat. One effective method is the practice of deep, focused breathing. When you feel the tide of panic rising, pause and breathe deeply, counting slowly to five as you inhale and again to five as you exhale. This simple act can significantly reduce immediate anxiety by lowering your heart rate and signaling to your brain that you are not in immediate danger, thus shifting your body out of its fight-or-flight response.

Another powerful technique is grounding yourself in the present moment through sensory engagement. This involves paying close attention to your immediate environment and engaging all your senses—what you can see, hear, touch, taste, and smell. This practice not only diverts your attention from distressing thoughts but also helps anchor you in the here and now, reducing feelings of detachment or unreality that intense anxiety can sometimes provoke.

Visualization also plays a crucial role in self-soothing. When fears of abandonment grip you, visualize a place where you feel safe and calm. Imagine yourself there, and focus on the details of this safe haven—the colors, the sounds, and how calm you feel within this space. This mental escape can provide a brief break, allowing you to regain your emotional balance.

Building Internal Security

Developing a sense of security from within is perhaps the most significant step toward overcoming the fear of abandonment. This internal security is a quiet assurance, a deep-seated belief in your own worth and resilience, independent of external validation. Building this starts with challenging and changing the negative self-beliefs that often accompany abandonment issues. Replace thoughts like "I am not enough" or "I will always be left" with affirmations that reinforce your value and strength. Regularly engaging in activities that bolster your confidence and self-esteem can further reinforce this internal security. Whether it's through mastering a new skill, dedicating time to passions that ignite your spirit, or simply through routines that nurture your physical and mental health, these practices build a foundation of self-respect and self-assuredness.

Journaling is another tool that can enhance your internal security. By writing about your feelings of abandonment and the triggers that ignite these feelings, you can gain clearer insights into the patterns of your emotional responses. This self-reflection fosters greater self-awareness, allowing you to confront and comfort the parts of yourself that are still haunted by the fear of being left.

Creating Trusting Relationships

The cornerstone of any thriving relationship is trust, without which the fear of abandonment can flourish unchecked. Building and maintaining trusting relationships starts with open, honest communication. Regularly share your thoughts, feelings, and fears with your partner, not as accusations but as shared truths, looking for mutual solutions. This openness can foster intimacy and understanding, showing you both that vulnerability can be met with support rather than withdrawal.

Being able to listen plays a crucial role in this process. Actively listen to your partner's concerns and feelings, validating them as legitimate and important. This mutual respect for each other's emotional worlds can strengthen the trust between you, gradually dismantling the walls built by abandonment fears.

Moreover, consistent behavior is key in creating trust. Be reliable in small things—calling when you say you will, showing up on time, following through on commitments. These actions, though seemingly small, can have a profound impact on building a sense of reliability and safety in your relationship. They demonstrate that you are present and invested, qualities that are essential in co-creating a secure, loving partnership where fears of abandonment can be viewed through the lens of compassion and understanding, rather than panic and pre-emption.

The Cycle of Push and Pull in Relationships

In the complex dance of relationships, those with anxious attachment often find themselves caught in a confusing rhythm of push and pull. This dynamic is characterized by alternating periods of intense closeness and sudden emotional withdrawal. On one hand, there is a profound desire for intimacy and connection, driving you to seek closeness with your partner aggressively. On the other hand, there's an overwhelming fear that this very closeness will inevitably lead to hurt or disappointment, prompting you to pull away in a protective response. This cycle can be bewildering not just for you but also for your partner, as they navigate through these conflicting signals without a clear understanding of what triggers them.

Understanding the underlying mechanics of this push-pull dynamic is crucial. It often stems from a battle between two conflicting internal dialogues. One voice craves closeness and assurance, driven by the fear of being alone or unloved. This voice pushes you towards your partner, seeking comfort and security in their presence. However, nearly as soon as this closeness is achieved, another voice chimes in—one that whispers warnings of impending rejection or abandonment, suggesting that it's safer to retreat before these fears manifest into reality. This internal conflict is not merely exhausting—it can cloud your perception of the relationship, distorting minor issues into potential threats.

These fears are often traced back to early relational blueprints laid down by interactions with significant caregivers. If those early relationships taught you that closeness could lead to pain—through inconsistent nurturing, conditional affection, or sudden emotional unavailability—you might subconsciously believe that all close relationships are fraught with the danger of hurting you. This belief, though rooted in past experiences, asserts itself in your current relationship dynamics, driving the push-pull behavior that so confuses the pattern of your romantic engagements.

The stability and security of your relationships can significantly suffer under the strain of this cycle. Each instance of pulling away can create confusion and hurt in your partner, leading them to question the viability and health of the relationship. From their perspective, the relationship might seem fraught with mixed signals and instability, which can erode trust and emotional safety over time. The unpredictable nature of the push-pull dynamic can inhibit the development of a steady, nurturing connection, making it challenging to build a future together based on mutual understanding and support.

Breaking free from this exhausting cycle involves a conscious effort to understand and manage the fears that fuel it. Begin by observing the moments when you feel the urge to pull away. What thoughts or feelings are surfacing? Are they factual, or are they projections of past fears onto your current relationship? Acknowledging these moments and understanding their triggers is the first step towards gaining control over them.

One effective strategy to manage these impulses is to practice open communication with your partner about your fears. This doesn't mean simply telling your partner when you're feeling scared or insecure; it involves sharing why you feel this way and what experiences have shaped these fears. Such vulnerability can seem daunting, but remember that allowing your partner to understand your triggers can help them to be more empathetic and supportive when these feelings overwhelm you.

Additionally, developing self-soothing strategies can empower you to handle these emotions independently without always relying on your partner. Practicing deep breathing, mindfulness meditation, or engaging in a hobby that absorbs your attention can help regulate your emotions, reducing the intensity of the urge to push your partner away. By strengthening your emotional self-sufficiency, you decrease the likelihood of your fears dictating your actions in the relationship.

Another vital part of breaking the cycle is to consciously make efforts to maintain closeness, even when your instinct is to withdraw. This might mean resisting the urge to cancel plans or to be physically distant. It involves reminding yourself that the feelings of safety and love you experience in moments of closeness are real and that your relationship is not doomed to follow old patterns. Regularly affirming the positive experiences and stable aspects of your relationship can also help counterbalance the fear-driven impulse to flee.

By understanding the push-pull dynamics and actively working to stabilize your emotional responses, you can foster a healthier, more consistent approach to intimacy. This not only enhances your relationship satisfaction but also contributes to a more profound sense of personal security and self-awareness, allowing you to engage in relationships with confidence and genuine openness.

People-Pleasing: When the Desire to be Liked Overwhelms

In the intricate web of human relationships, the tendency to consistently prioritize others' needs above your own—commonly known as people-pleasing—can often stem from an anxious attachment style. This behavior pattern isn't just about being kind or considerate; it's rooted in a deep-seated fear of rejection and a strong need for approval. People-pleasing often manifests as an overwhelming urge to ensure everyone else is happy, sometimes at the expense of your own emotional well-being.

Understanding what constitutes people-pleasing is essential. It involves more than simply being helpful or caring; it's a pattern where your actions are primarily driven by a desire to be liked or to avoid conflict at all costs. For instance, you might find yourself saying 'yes' to tasks you'd rather not do or going along with plans that don't interest you, all because you fear that asserting your preferences might lead others to dislike or reject you. This behavior is deeply intertwined with anxious attachment, as both share a fundamental fear of not being good enough or of being left alone.

The cost of such behavior is multifaceted, affecting both emotional health and relationship dynamics. Constantly putting others ahead of yourself can lead to burnout, resentment, and a weak sense of self-identity. Emotionally, it keeps you in a perpetual state of anxiety, as the stability of your relationships seems contingent on your ability to keep others happy. Relationally, it can create imbalances where your needs are perpetually sidelined, which can lead to unfulfilling or even exploitative relationships. Over time, this imbalance can erode the very connections you're striving to strengthen, as genuine intimacy is replaced with transactional interactions based on appeasement rather than mutual respect and affection.

Recognizing people-pleasing behaviors in yourself is the first step towards change. Reflect on recent interactions and ask yourself why you acted in a certain way. Was it truly out of care, or was there a fear of displeasing someone? Notice patterns where you might be agreeing to things reluctantly or where you feel unable to express your true feelings. It's also helpful to pay attention to feelings of resentment, which can be a strong indicator that you're overextending yourself to please others.

Transitioning to healthier interpersonal dynamics requires a balance —a move from compulsive people-pleasing to healthy assertiveness. This shift begins with establishing boundaries, which involves understanding and communicating your limits and needs clearly. Start small, perhaps by saying 'no' to minor requests that you would typically agree to out of obligation. Explain your reasons honestly, which can help others understand your perspective and gradually adjust their expectations.

Developing assertiveness also means learning to tolerate the discomfort that sometimes comes with not meeting everyone's expectations. It involves internal work, particularly around self-worth. Remind yourself that your value does not diminish because someone is displeased with your actions. Building this internal resilience can empower you to make choices that are true to your needs and values, rather than choices aimed merely at securing approval.

Finally, fostering healthier dynamics involves nurturing relationships where mutual respect and reciprocity are the norms. Seek out and nurture connections with individuals who appreciate your authenticity and who encourage you to express your thoughts and needs openly. In such relationships, you'll find that being loved and valued doesn't require you to lose yourself in the process. Instead, it involves a shared journey of growth and understanding, where both parties feel seen, heard, and valued for who they truly are.

As we conclude this exploration of people-pleasing and its impact on those with anxious attachment styles, we recognize the profound influence that fear and a desire for approval can have on personal interactions. By understanding the roots of people-pleasing, recognizing its costs, and taking steps towards healthier interpersonal dynamics, you can start to create connections that are not only more fulfilling but also more balanced and genuine. This process is not just about changing how you interact with others; it's about transforming how you view yourself and what you believe you deserve in relationships. Moving forward, the focus will shift to deeper strategies that address these issues, providing you with tools to enhance not only your relationships but also your sense of self-worth and personal fulfillment.

Chapter 3

Building Self-Esteem and Independence

As you continue to navigate through the layers of understanding your anxious attachment style, a crucial aspect that often emerges is the concept of self-esteem—how you perceive and value yourself in the absence of external validation. For many, the roots of anxious attachment are tangled up with self-worth, where feelings of value are inextricably linked to the affirmations and actions of others. This chapter is dedicated to untangling these roots, guiding you toward cultivating a robust sense of self-worth that stands independent of the opinions and reactions of those around you.

Cultivating Self-Worth: Exercises and Strategies

Identify Your Strengths

One of the most transformative exercises for enhancing self-esteem involves a deep dive into recognizing your personal strengths and achievements. This practice is about shifting focus from what you perceive as deficits or areas of dependency, to acknowledging and celebrating your unique talents and accomplishments. Start by listing out moments in your life where you felt particularly proud of an achievement or when others recognized your abilities. These can range from small successes, like completing a challenging project at work or managing to keep calm in a stressful situation, to significant milestones, such as earning a degree or mastering a new skill.

This exercise not only reminds you of your capabilities but also helps rewire any persistent negative thoughts that may suggest you are not good enough unless validated by someone else. Reflecting on your strengths reinforces the understanding that your worth is not a derivative of other people's approval but a celebration of your own intrinsic qualities and efforts.

Positive Affirmations

Positive affirmations are powerful because they help reshape your internal dialogue, particularly if your self-talk has been skewed by years of insecurity and dependence on external validation. Affirmations are positive, empowering statements that, when repeated often, can help you internalize feelings of self-worth and confidence. For example, affirmations like "I am worthy of love and respect," "My feelings are valid," or "I trust in my ability to overcome these challenges" are not just words but powerful mantras that can fortify your belief in your own value.

Incorporate these affirmations into your daily routine—say them out loud every morning, write them in your journal, or post them in places where you'll see them throughout the day. Over time, these affirmations can help shift the narrative from uncertainty about your worth to a more confident and secure understanding of yourself.

Setting Achievable Goals

Another vital strategy in building self-esteem involves setting and achieving personal goals. Goals give you a sense of direction and purpose, something that is especially important if you've felt lost or dependent on others for emotional guidance. Start with small, realistic goals to avoid feeling overwhelmed. These could be as simple as reading a book a month, going for a daily walk, or learning a new recipe each week. Achieving these goals provides a tangible sense of accomplishment that boosts your self-esteem and reinforces your capabilities.

The key is to choose meaningful goals rather than those you think you should pursue to impress or please others. This shift not only fosters independence but also aligns your actions more closely with your personal values and interests, further enhancing your sense of self-worth.

Self-Worth vs. External Validation

Finally, an essential aspect of building self-esteem is learning to distinguish between self-worth and external validation. While it's natural to enjoy and appreciate recognition from others, a healthy sense of self-worth should not be predominantly dependent on it. Begin by consciously recognizing moments when you seek external validation, especially when it's about making important decisions or assessing your own achievements. Ask yourself, "Am I choosing this because it feels right for me or because I want others to see me in a certain light?"

Gradually, work on trusting your own judgments and feelings more than the opinions of others. This doesn't mean you ignore constructive feedback or the feelings of people you care about; it simply means that you give your own insights and emotions the attention and respect they deserve. This practice can help solidify your self-esteem, making it less vulnerable to the fluctuations of other people's perceptions and more a reflection of your true self.

Through these exercises and strategies, you can embark on a profound path toward recognizing and reinforcing your self-worth.

This journey is about more than just feeling good about yourself—it's about establishing a foundation of self-respect and independence that will enrich not only your relationships but every area of your life. As you continue to cultivate this robust sense of self, remember that each step forward is a step toward a more empowered and fulfilled you, one where your worth is defined not by others but by your own deep sense of self-respect and accomplishment.

Embracing Solitude: Finding Strength in Being Alone

In the quiet moments of solitude, you might initially confront a wave of unease, a sense that being alone is akin to being lonely or abandoned. Yet, a profound strength and self-discovery is waiting on the far side of that discomfort—a reclamation of your inner peace and self-reliance that can only emerge when you are by yourself. Transforming solitude from a state of loneliness to a powerful tool for healing and self-discovery begins with a shift in perspective. It involves seeing these quiet moments not as a void to be filled with the presence of others, but as a precious space where the deepest parts of you can unfold and reveal themselves.

Solitude offers a unique environment where the noise of external expectations and social dynamics falls away, leaving you with the pure essence of your thoughts and feelings. This setting is invaluable for fostering a deep connection with yourself, allowing you to engage in introspection and self-reflection without distractions. It is here, in the silence of your own company, where you can truly listen to your own needs, desires, and emotions. This practice is not about isolating yourself from loved ones but about balancing your social interactions with moments where you can return to your core, recenter, and cultivate a grounded sense of self that enhances your interactions with others.

Mindfulness and Solitude

Integrating mindfulness into your periods of solitude can significantly enhance the benefits of this time alone. Mindfulness— the practice of being fully present in the moment—helps anchor you in the here and now, removing worries about the past or anxieties about the future. It allows you to experience solitude as a state of being rather than a condition of lack. Simple mindfulness techniques like focus breathing, observing your thoughts without judgment, or engaging deeply with your current activity can transform your experience of being alone from one of loneliness to one of enriching solitude.

You might start with a mindfulness walk, where you focus solely on the experience of walking, noticing the sensation of your feet touching the floor, the rhythm of your breath, and the sounds around you. This practice not only provides the benefits of physical activity but also helps you cultivate a mindful presence that can carry over into other areas of your life. Similarly, sitting quietly with a cup of tea and allowing yourself to be fully engaged with the experience— the warmth of the cup, the aroma of the tea, the flavors on your tongue— can be a form of mindfulness that enriches your moments of solitude.

Activities to Enjoy Alone

The activities you choose to engage in during your moments of solitude can also play a significant role in enhancing your self-discovery and happiness. Consider activities that resonate with your personal interests and passions, perhaps those you've put aside due to a busy schedule or social obligations. This could be anything from painting, writing, gardening, or playing a musical instrument to more reflective practices like journaling or reading. These activities not only provide pleasure and a sense of accomplishment but also foster a deeper connection with your inner self, allowing your creativity and thoughts to flow freely without concern for external judgment or interruption.

Engaging in creative activities alone can be particularly therapeutic. Creativity is inherently exploratory, a way of communicating with the deepest parts of yourself. It allows you to express your bottled emotions and thoughts that might be hard to articulate in words, providing a tangible outlet for your inner experiences. Whether you're creating art, writing poetry, or crafting, these activities can be powerful tools for self-expression and self-understanding.

Building Comfort with Being Alone

For many people, especially those with an anxious attachment style, building comfort with being alone is a gradual process. It involves gently stretching the boundaries of your comfort zone and taking small steps toward embracing solitude without overwhelming yourself. Start with short periods of alone time, slowly increasing the duration as you become more comfortable. During these times, engage in activities that you genuinely enjoy, which can help shift the experience of being alone from something to endure to something to look forward to.

It's also helpful to create a comforting and inviting space for your solitude. This might mean decorating a corner of your home with items that bring you joy and comfort—a cozy chair, soft lighting, pleasant scents, or soothing music. This physical space can then become a sanctuary for your solo time, a physical representation of the welcoming nature of solitude.

As you become more accustomed to and comfortable with being alone, you may start to notice a shift in how you view solitude. What once might have felt like a daunting expanse of time can transform into a cherished opportunity for growth and self-reflection. This newfound appreciation for solitude not only enriches your life but also enhances your relationships as you bring a more whole and centered self to your interactions with others. Embracing solitude, therefore, is not just about finding peace in being alone but about building a stronger, more resilient self that thrives in both solitude and company.

Developing a Secure Sense of Self

In the quest to cultivate a secure sense of self, it's crucial to delve deeply into the exploration of your personal values, interests, and aspirations. This deep dive is not merely an academic exercise but a profound journey into understanding what truly motivates, fulfills, and resonates with your deepest self. By identifying these core aspects, you not only carve out a niche of self-identity that is uniquely yours but also anchor your sense of self in attributes and values that are not easily shaken by external fluctuations. Start by asking yourself questions like, "What values do I hold dear?" and "What activities bring me genuine joy?" or "What aspirations have I sidelined or not pursued due to fear or insecurity?" Engage with these questions through writing, reflection, or creative expression, allowing yourself the space and freedom to explore these aspects without judgment.

This exploration helps in solidifying your self-identity, which is especially beneficial if you've previously found yourself molding your interests or values to match those of others, a common scenario in those with an anxious attachment style. For example, if you've always adapted your hobbies to align with a partner's or sought approval by embracing values that aren't genuinely your own, this exploration can be particularly liberating. It's about reclaiming your individuality and recognizing that your interests and values are worthy of space and expression, irrespective of how others perceive them.

The journey towards a secure self also involves addressing and reducing emotional dependency on others. Dependency often arises from a fear of not being enough by yourself, which can lead to constantly seeking out others for validation or company. To counter this, start by assessing situations where you feel most dependent on others for emotional support or decision-making. Gradually, begin to practice making small decisions independently, trusting your judgment and intuition. Simultaneously, engage more frequently in activities that you can do alone, which reinforces your capability and reduces the anxiety associated with solitude. This practice not only fosters a sense of independence but also enhances your confidence in your ability to manage life's challenges without excessive reliance on others.

Moreover, the role of self-reflection in this process cannot be overstated. Reflective practices such as journaling or meditation offer you a mirror to your internal world, helping you to understand and affirm your beliefs, desires, and fears. Regular self-reflection can illuminate patterns in your thoughts and behavior, some of which may be contributing to a shaky sense of self. For instance, you might discover through reflection that you tend to downplay your accomplishments or shy away from expressing your needs. Recognizing such patterns is the first step in modifying them. Use this insight to consciously practice acknowledging your achievements and asserting your needs, which are integral actions for nurturing a secure sense of self.

Lastly, embracing change and personal growth is integral to developing a secure sense of self. Change is often daunting, especially if you've found a semblance of safety in predictability and routine, which can be comforting if your attachment style has left you wary of uncertainty. However, growth inherently involves stepping into new experiences and challenges. Start by setting small, manageable goals for personal development, whether in your skills, knowledge, or emotional resilience. Treat each step into new territory not as a potential threat but as an opportunity for enrichment and self-discovery. As you accumulate experiences that affirm your ability to adapt and thrive amidst change, your self-identity will begin to integrate these strengths, reinforcing a self-image that is confident and secure.

Through these practices, you are not just building a robust sense of self but are also laying down a foundation where anxious attachment no longer dictates your interactions and choices. This foundation supports not only healthier relationships but also a life where decisions are guided by a clear understanding and acceptance of your true self. As you continue to engage in these practices, let each new discovery about yourself remind you of your journey towards a life defined not by fear or dependency but by confidence and authenticity.

The Fear of Missing Out in Relationships

In a world where social media often acts as a highlight reel of other's lives, the fear of missing out—commonly known as FOMO—can seep into our personal relationships, subtly influencing how we perceive our own interactions and commitments. This phenomenon isn't just about envying others' experiences or social gatherings; it extends into how we measure our relationships against those we see online or hear about from friends, often leading to unnecessary dissatisfaction and unrest. For people with an anxious attachment style, this can exacerbate feelings of insecurity and inadequacy, making it crucial to recognize and address the triggers of FOMO in your relationships.

The first step in managing FOMO is recognizing what specifically triggers these feelings for you. It might be scrolling through social media and seeing friends or acquaintances sharing moments with their significant others that seem more romantic or exciting than your own experiences. Or, it could be hearing friends discuss their relationships in ways that highlight aspects absent in yours, such as constant adventure or seemingly perfect communication. These triggers can often lead to a spiral of comparison and doubt, where you question the quality and depth of your own relationships based not on your actual experiences but on an idealized version of others' highlights.

To combat this, it's essential to critically assess the role of social media and external narratives in shaping your perception of relationship success. Remember, what is shared publicly is often curated and represents only a fraction of the reality of those relationships. Reducing the time spent on social media apps or altering how you engage with them can significantly lessen the intensity of FOMO feelings. Consider unfollowing accounts or limiting exposure to feeds that often trigger feelings of inadequacy or jealousy, replacing them with content that uplifts or resonates more authentically with your values and real-world experiences.

Finding Contentment in the Present

Another vital aspect of overcoming FOMO is learning to find joy and contentment in your present circumstances and relationships. This involves a deliberate shift of focus from what might be lacking to appreciating what is present and thriving. Begin by making a daily or weekly list of moments or aspects of your relationship that brought you happiness, comfort, or pride. These don't have to be grand gestures or milestone events; simple joys like enjoying a quiet morning together, a thoughtful conversation, or a shared laugh over an inside joke are equally significant.

Engaging fully in the present also means practicing mindfulness in your interactions with your partner. This can be as easy as actively listening when they speak without planning your next response or allowing your mind to wander to other things you could be doing. By being fully present, you not only enrich your own experience but also strengthen the connection within your relationship, making each moment together more meaningful and satisfying.

Balancing Social Life and Self-Care

Balancing your social engagements with personal downtime is crucial in managing FOMO, especially for those prone to overcommitting socially, as a way to avoid feeling left out or alone. This balance is not about withdrawing from social activities but about integrating them in a way that doesn't compromise your well-being or the health of your relationship. It involves recognizing when to say no to invitations, understanding that it's okay to prioritize quiet, personal time over social gatherings, and respecting your own needs as much as you respect others.

Incorporating regular self-care routines can significantly aid in this balance. Self-care can be different for everyone, from physical activities that help lower stress, such as yoga or hiking, to quiet, introspective practices like reading, meditating, or journaling. These activities not only provide a needed break from social stimuli but also help ground your thoughts and emotions, reducing the impact of FOMO and enhancing your overall mental and emotional resilience.

As you implement these strategies, you may find that the fear of missing out becomes less compelling, overshadowed by a growing appreciation for your own life and relationships as they are, not as they compare to others. This shift is not about settling or lowering expectations but about cultivating a deeper, more grounded perspective that values honest, lived experiences over perceived ideals. In doing so, you not only free yourself from the constant chase after what others have but also open up space to genuinely enjoy and nurture the relationships that matter most to you.

From Self-Criticism to Self-Compassion

When the voice inside your head is harsher than anyone you might encounter in your daily life, it's time to consider whether self-criticism is serving you or simply sabotaging your happiness and relationships. Often, self-criticism stems from an internalized pressure to meet often unrealistic standards, a trait that can be particularly pronounced if you grapple with an anxious attachment style. This harsh self-talk can keep you in a perpetual state of feeling 'not good enough,' affecting not only your mental health but also how you interact with others, making relationships fraught with unnecessary tension.

The damage inflicted by excessive self-criticism goes beyond fleeting feelings of inadequacy; it can engrain a cycle of negative self-perception that impacts all areas of life. In relationships, it might manifest as constant fear that you are not living up to the expectations of your partner or that you must earn their love and approval continuously. This mindset not only strains your interactions but can also stop you from fully experiencing the joy and love available to you. In your personal life, this relentless self-critique can hurt your ability to take risks or embrace opportunities for fear of failure or not measuring up.

Transitioning from self-criticism to self-compassion is not merely a nice-to-have but a necessary shift for fostering healthier relationships and a happier life. Self-compassion is about treating yourself with the kindness, concern, and support you would show to a good friend. To cultivate this, start by recognizing moments of self-criticism and consciously choosing to silence that critical inner voice. Instead, offer yourself words of encouragement and understanding. For instance, if you catch yourself mentally replaying moments where you believe you fell short, gently remind yourself that everyone makes mistakes and that each error is a step toward growth.

Practicing Self-Compassion

Practicing self-compassion can be transformative, acting as a balm to the often self-inflicted wounds of harsh self-judgment. Begin by incorporating basic self-compassion exercises into your daily routine. One effective technique is to write a letter to yourself from the perspective of a close, compassionate friend. In this letter, address your perceived shortcomings or failures with empathy, understanding, and encouragement. This exercise not only helps externalize your self-critical thoughts but also helps you internalize a more compassionate viewpoint.

Another powerful method is the 'self-compassion break,' a practice you can use whenever you find yourself in the throes of self-criticism. Simply pause, place your hand on your heart, and acknowledge your feelings of inadequacy or disappointment as a natural part of being human. Offer yourself comforting words, such as, "It's okay to feel this way; it's part of being human," or "May I give myself the compassion that I need." This physical gesture of placing a hand over your heart can be surprisingly soothing and acts as a physical reminder to treat yourself with care.

Reframing Negative Thoughts

Reframing negative thoughts is another crucial aspect of developing self-compassion. This cognitive behavioral technique involves identifying negative, often automatic thoughts and challenging their validity. For instance, if you find yourself thinking, "I always mess things up," try to reframe that thought to something more balanced and kind, such as, "Sometimes I make mistakes, but I also have many successes." This practice of reframing doesn't mean ignoring your faults but rather viewing your experiences through a lens that is not distorted by overly harsh criticism.

As you practice reframing your thoughts, you'll notice a shift in your internal dialogue, becoming more supportive and less punitive. This change can significantly affect how you feel about yourself and interact with others, leading to improved self-esteem and healthier relationships.

Celebrating Personal Progress

Finally, make it a habit to celebrate your progress, no matter how small. Each step you take towards being more compassionate with yourself is a victory worth recognizing. Celebrate these moments by acknowledging your effort, perhaps by journaling about your experiences or sharing your progress with a supportive friend. These celebrations can reinforce the positive changes you're making and motivate you to continue on this path.

Incorporating self-compassion into your life allows for a softer, more accepting relationship with yourself, which in turn, enriches your relationships with others. By reducing self-criticism and increasing self-compassion, you not only enhance your own well-being but also create a more loving and accepting space for your relationships to thrive.

As this chapter closes, remember that the journey to replacing self-criticism with self-compassion is both challenging and rewarding. It requires patience, persistence, and most importantly, a willingness to treat yourself with kindness. In doing so, you open up a new way of interacting with the world, one that is characterized by greater peace, acceptance, and genuine connection.

Chapter 4

Emotional Regulation and Mindfulness

Mindfulness, a simple yet profound tool, offers a way to cultivate this inner stillness, enabling you to engage with life's emotional upheavals with a sense of clarity and calm. In this chapter, we explore how mindfulness can not only soothe relationship anxiety but transform the way you connect with yourself and others.

Mindfulness Practices for Relationship Anxiety

Introduction to Mindfulness

Mindfulness is the art of maintaining a present awareness of our thoughts, feelings, body, and surroundings with openness, curiosity, and acceptance. Think of it as tuning into a frequency that connects you deeply with the present moment rather than getting lost in regrets about the past or worries about the future. This practice is particularly valuable if you struggle with anxious attachment, as it helps break the cycle of fear that often clouds your relationship experiences. By fostering mindfulness, you learn to respond to relationship dynamics based on present interactions instead of reacting through the lens of past insecurities or future fears.

Mindfulness Meditation

One of the most effective ways to cultivate mindfulness is through meditation. To practice Mindfulness meditation, you need to sit quietly and pay attention to your thoughts, sounds, breathing, and parts of the body. It's about observing without criticism, allowing your thoughts and feelings to come and go without getting entangled in them. Start with just five minutes a day, and gradually increase the time as you feel more comfortable with the practice.

Here's a simple mindfulness meditation you can try:

1. Find a quiet and comfortable place to sit down.
2. Close your eyes and take a few deep breaths.
3. Begin to focus your attention on your breath—the inhale and exhale.
4. When your mind wanders, as it will, gently return your focus to your breathing.
5. Continue this for several minutes, observing your breath and the sensations in your body.

This technique is simple and can have a deep impact on your emotional state. It teaches you to bring your attention back to the present whenever you find yourself spiraling into anxieties about your relationships.

Being Present in Relationships

The practice of being present or fully engaging with the here and now in your relationships can significantly deepen your connections. When you are truly present with a partner, you listen more deeply, respond more thoughtfully, and engage more authentically. This presence can be particularly challenging if you have an anxious attachment style, as you might often find yourself distracted by worries or insecurities. Mindfulness cultivates a kind of mental discipline, training you to keep your attention on the current interaction and not on the myriad "what ifs" that your mind might generate.

Mindfulness in Communication

Applying mindfulness to communication involves being fully present during conversations, which allows for more genuine dialogue and fosters greater understanding and empathy. It means really listening to what your partner is saying without planning your next response or interpreting their words through a filter of anxiety. This can be practiced by focusing intently on the conversation, noting the feelings and thoughts that arise but choosing to let them pass without immediate reaction. This approach not only reduces misunderstandings but also enhances the emotional depth of your interactions.

To integrate mindfulness into your communication:

- Focus on listening rather than thinking about what you will say next.
- If you notice yourself becoming reactive or defensive, take a pause, breathe, and bring your focus back to the discussion.
- Try to identify the emotion behind your partner's words instead of just the words themselves.

By weaving mindfulness into your daily interactions, you not only improve your relationships but also transform your engagement with the world. It allows you to move through life with a greater sense of peace, grounded in the richness of the present moment, rather than being perpetually tossed by the waves of past regrets or future worries.

Identifying Triggers: A Guide to Emotional Awareness

In exploring the landscape of your emotions, especially when dealing with an anxious attachment style, understanding what specific situations or behaviors trigger your anxious responses can be illuminating. These triggers are like silent alarms that set off your anxiety, often rooted in deep-seated fears or past experiences. Identifying these triggers is crucial because it allows you to anticipate and prepare for emotional reactions rather than being caught off-guard. Each trigger, whether it's a tone of voice, a particular phrase, a type of interaction, or even specific dates, carries with it a story—a story of past pain, disappointment, or insecurity. By recognizing these triggers, you not only gain insight into the workings of your emotional responses but also empower yourself to handle these situations with greater awareness and control.

For example, consider a scenario where you find yourself feeling unusually anxious when your partner does not immediately respond to your text messages. This reaction could stem from a deeper fear of abandonment or neglect, perhaps echoing times in past relationships or childhood when emotional support was inconsistent or conditional. In recognizing this pattern, you can begin to differentiate between the present reality and the past fears influencing your reactions. This understanding provides a vital space between trigger and response, where choices lie—a space where you can decide how to react in ways that align with your current relationship goals and personal growth.

Journaling for Emotional Clarity

One effective tool for tracking and understanding your emotional triggers is journaling. This practice offers a private, unfiltered medium where you can express and explore the nuances of your feelings. Start by keeping a daily log of instances where you feel heightened anxiety or insecurity, noting what happened, how you felt, and what you think might have triggered those feelings. Over time, patterns will likely emerge, highlighting specific triggers and your typical reactions to them.

To deepen this exploration, you can use journal prompts designed to uncover layers of emotional triggers. Questions like, "What memories come to mind when I feel abandoned?" or "What am I really afraid of when I feel jealous?" can guide you in tracing the roots of your triggers. This practice not only enhances your self-awareness but also aids in processing and healing old wounds that may be contributing to your current emotional landscape.

The Role of Therapy

While journaling and self-reflection are powerful tools, the role of therapy in identifying and managing emotional triggers cannot be overstated. Therapy provides a professional and supportive setting where you can explore your triggers with guidance from someone who can offer insights and techniques that are perhaps not accessible on your own. A therapist can help you connect the dots between your past experiences and current reactions, offering strategies tailored to your specific needs. They can also provide support as you work through the sometimes painful memories or fears associated with these triggers, making the process of understanding and healing less daunting.

In therapy, practices such as Cognitive Behavioral Therapy (CBT) are often used to address the thoughts and behaviors linked to emotional triggers. Through CBT, you can learn to question and reframe the negative thought patterns that triggers can activate, reducing their power to dictate your emotional responses. This kind of therapeutic work can be transformative, providing you not just relief from symptoms but also a pathway to deeper emotional freedom and resilience.

Preventive Strategies

Equipped with an understanding of your triggers and the tools to manage them, you can develop preventive strategies that allow you to navigate potential trigger situations with greater ease and confidence. One effective strategy is the creation of a personalized plan that outlines specific steps you will take when you encounter a trigger. This plan might include pausing to use mindfulness techniques, employing calming breathwork, reaching out to a supportive friend or partner, or using affirmations that reinforce your security and worth.

Another preventive strategy involves setting boundaries in relationships or situations that you know are likely to trigger your anxiety. This might mean communicating your needs more clearly, such as asking for regular check-ins with a partner in a long-distance relationship or setting limits around discussions of topics that tend to trigger insecurity. By establishing and maintaining these boundaries, you not only protect your emotional health but also build relationships that are more supportive and understanding of your needs.

Understanding and managing your emotional triggers is a crucial step in cultivating a healthier, more secure attachment style. It requires patience, honesty, and, often, the willingness to confront and work through painful memories or fears. But the rewards—a deeper understanding of yourself, more fulfilling relationships, and a greater sense of emotional peace—are profound. As you continue to explore and apply these insights, remember that each step forward enriches not only your relationships but also your journey toward a more secure and joyful life.

Self-Soothing Techniques for Immediate Relief

In the midst of emotional turbulence, especially when triggered by the intense fears and uncertainties characteristic of anxious attachment, finding immediate ways to regain a sense of calm and control is crucial. This is where self-soothing techniques come into play, serving as practical tools to stabilize your emotions on the spot. Let's explore how breathwork and sensory engagement can serve as your allies in restoring peace and equilibrium during moments of distress.

Basics of Breathwork

Breathwork is a collection of various techniques that involve consciously manipulating your breathing pattern to influence your mental, emotional, and physical state. It's rooted in the principle that breathing is uniquely both a voluntary and involuntary system; it bridges the body's autonomic (involuntary) functions and our conscious control. This dual nature of breathing makes it a powerful tool for regulating physiological and emotional responses to stress. When you alter your breath, you signal your body to shift from a state of alertness and anxiety—often characterized by shallow, rapid breathing—to a state of relaxation and calm, marked by deeper, slower breaths. This shift can help deactivate the body's stress response and activate the relaxation response, helping to alleviate immediate symptoms of anxiety.

Breathing Techniques

There are several breathing techniques you can employ for immediate relief from stress and anxiety, each tailored to different emotional states:

- Deep Breathing: This practice involves taking slow, deep breaths through the nose, allowing your abdomen to expand as your lungs fill with air, and then exhaling slowly through the mouth. This technique is particularly effective for combating acute stress and helping to center your thoughts when you feel overwhelmed.

- 4-7-8 Breathing: Also known as the "Relaxing Breath." To do this, you need to breathe in for 4 seconds, hold your breath for 7 seconds, and exhale for 8 seconds. 4-7-8 is beneficial for reducing anxiety and helping you to fall asleep, as it promotes a greater sense of control over your breath and, by extension, your current state of mind.
- Alternate Nostril Breathing: This technique, which comes from the yogic tradition, involves closing one nostril while inhaling through the other, then closing the other nostril and exhaling through the first. This is repeated for several cycles. Alternate nostril breathing is ideal for restoring balance and calm, particularly if you're feeling emotionally scattered or agitated.

Sensory Engagement Methods

Engaging your senses deliberately can also serve as a powerful method for emotional regulation. By focusing your attention on sensory experiences, you draw your mind away from distressing thoughts and anchor it in the present moment, reducing feelings of anxiety or overwhelm. Here are a few sensory engagement methods:

- Touch: Techniques like holding a piece of ice, feeling the texture of a fabric, or even petting an animal can dramatically shift your focus. The physical sensation provides a distraction from distressing emotions and helps ground you in the here and now.
- Smell: Aromatherapy has long been used for its calming effects. Scents like lavender, chamomile, or sandalwood can be soothing. Keeping a small bottle of essential oil or a scented handkerchief can be a quick way to engage this sense when you need to calm your mind.

Emotional Grounding Techniques

Grounding techniques are designed to help you detach from emotional pain and connect to the external world. For instance:

- 5-4-3-2-1 Technique: This involves identifying five things you can see, four you can touch, three you can hear, two you can smell, and one you can taste. It's an effective method for pulling your mind away from the source of stress and redirecting it towards external stimuli.
- Mental Grounding: This involves focusing on a mental task like listing all states in alphabetical order or counting backward from 100 by sevens. The concentration required allows you to shift your mental state away from anxiety and towards the task at hand.

Creating a Self-Soothing Kit

To have these tools readily available, consider creating a personal self-soothing kit. This kit might include items like a stress ball, essential oils for aromatherapy, a small notebook and pen for journaling or doodling, calming tea bags, and perhaps a USB with a pre-loaded guided meditation or soothing music. Having these items gathered in one place ensures that you can quickly access them when feelings of anxiety strike, providing immediate tools to help manage your emotions effectively.

By integrating these self-soothing techniques into your routine, you equip yourself with practical strategies to navigate moments of anxiety or emotional overwhelm. Whether through breathwork, sensory engagement, or grounding exercises, these methods offer a pathway to regain control of your emotional state, fostering a sense of calm and stability even amidst the challenges of an anxious attachment style.

Cultivating Emotional Resilience

In the ever-changing landscape of our emotional lives, especially when navigating the complexities of relationships, emotional resilience serves as a vital skill, much like a deeply rooted tree that bends in the storm but does not break. Understanding emotional resilience involves recognizing it as the ability to quickly recover from difficulties and bounce back into shape, emotionally speaking. It's not about avoiding pain or hardship but about facing life's inevitable challenges with a spirit that is prepared not only to survive but to grow from the experience. This resilience is particularly crucial if you tend to feel overwhelmed by your anxieties or if your attachment style has left you vulnerable to the ebbs and flows of emotional tides in relationships.

Developing emotional resilience is a multi-faceted process that involves a series of intentional strategies. One of the first steps is to embrace challenges as opportunities for growth. This perspective shift is fundamental. Instead of viewing difficult situations or relationship conflicts as threats, seeing them as chances to strengthen your emotional muscles can change how you experience and respond to these events. Each challenge, while perhaps uncomfortable or painful, becomes a lesson in endurance and adaptability, teaching you more about your strengths and areas for improvement. For instance, a conflict with a partner might initially trigger your anxiety, but approaching this situation as an opportunity to better your communication skills and strengthen your understanding of each other's needs can turn a potentially negative experience into a growth opportunity.

Another crucial strategy in building resilience is learning from failures, which are inevitable parts of life. It's important to reframe how you view failure; rather than seeing it as a reflection of your worth or abilities, view it as a valuable source of insight. Analyzing what went wrong, what you could do differently next time, and what you learned are all parts of extracting value from failure. This approach not only softens the impact of the failure but also integrates it into your life as a stepping stone rather than a roadblock. For example, suppose a relationship ends despite your best efforts instead of spiraling into self-blame. In that case, you can take time to reflect on the dynamics of the relationship, recognize patterns that might have contributed to its decline, and plan ways to address these patterns in future relationships.

The role of a support system in building emotional resilience cannot be overstated. Humans are, by nature, social creatures, and our connections with others play a pivotal role in how we navigate life's ups and downs. A strong, supportive network of friends, family, or even colleagues provides emotional cushioning during times of stress or disappointment. These relationships offer perspectives that can challenge your own, support that can uplift you, and understanding that can comfort you. It's crucial to cultivate these relationships actively, investing time and energy into building bonds that are not only enjoyable but also resilient. This might mean reaching out for help when you need it, offering support when others are struggling, or simply engaging in regular, meaningful conversations that strengthen these emotional ties.

Resilience is not only about bouncing back but also about bouncing forward. It is about using the experience of recovery to propel yourself into a better understanding and functioning in the future. This aspect of resilience is particularly relevant when dealing with relationship setbacks or personal disappointments. Each setback carries with it the seeds of future growth if approached with the right mindset. For instance, recovering from a breakup or a significant disappointment can lead to deeper self-awareness, a clearer understanding of your relationship needs, and greater emotional strength, all of which can prepare you for more fulfilling relationships in the future. The key is to view recovery not just as getting back to where you were but as an opportunity to arrive at a new, more resilient place.

Cultivating emotional resilience is an ongoing process, one that requires patience, commitment, and a proactive approach to facing life's challenges. It involves continuously learning, adapting, and growing from every experience, supported by the knowledge that each step, no matter how difficult, is a step towards becoming a more emotionally robust individual. As you integrate these strategies into your life, your ability to deal with the complexities of relationships and personal challenges with grace and strength will inevitably enhance, paving the way for a more resilient, fulfilling life experience.

Breaking Free from the Overthinking Loop

The labyrinth of your thoughts can sometimes feel like a maze you've wandered into by accident, finding yourself looping back to the same worries and fears, no matter which way you turn. This pattern, known as overthinking, can be especially pervasive if you're grappling with anxious attachment, where every conversation and interaction is replayed and scrutinized for hidden meanings and potential threats. Recognizing when you've entered this mental maze is the first crucial step toward finding your way out. You might notice it happening when you're unable to sleep, ruminating over a comment made earlier in the day, or when you're feeling paralyzed by decision-making, trapped by the web of possible outcomes you can't stop envisioning.

The awareness of being caught in an overthinking loop is itself a beacon of hope. It signals that you have the self-awareness necessary to recognize these patterns, an essential skill in redirecting your mental energy more constructively. Start by observing these moments as they arise, noting what triggered the overthinking and the specific fears or anxieties driving it. Is it fear of a relationship failing or perhaps dread of not living up to someone's expectations? Pinpointing the root cause can demystify the overwhelming emotions and lead to more targeted strategies for intervention.

Interrupting the cycle of overthinking requires a toolkit of strategies designed to break the loop and redirect your thoughts. One effective technique involves setting a timer whenever you find yourself spiraling into overthinking. Give yourself a limited amount of time, say five minutes, to really delve into your worries. Once the timer goes off, consciously decide to move your focus onto a structured activity that requires your attention. This could be anything from a physical task like organizing your workspace to a cognitive one like solving a puzzle or planning your week. The key is to engage in an activity that absorbs your concentration, effectively shifting your mental gears away from rumination.

Another strategy is to practice "thought stopping," a cognitive intervention in which you mentally or even verbally command yourself to stop overthinking when you recognize it happening. This might involve visualizing a stop sign or mentally telling yourself "stop" and then purposefully replacing the overthought concern with a predetermined positive affirmation or constructive thought. For instance, replace thoughts of "What if I said something wrong?" with "I communicate honestly and clearly. I can clarify if there's a misunderstanding."

Mindfulness, a practice you've become familiar with in this journey, also plays a pivotal role in managing overthinking. It teaches you to watch your thoughts and emotions without attachment, viewing them as passing clouds in the sky of your mind. This perspective can reduce the urgency and intensity of overthinking, fostering a calm detachment that diffuses anxiety. Regular mindfulness practice, whether through meditation, mindful walking, or simply pausing to engage fully with the present moment, can strengthen your ability to remain centered amidst the whirlwind of your thoughts.

Creating a plan of action to address the concerns at the root of your overthinking can also be incredibly empowering. This involves shifting from a passive to an active stance, from worrying about what might happen to taking steps to deal with what actually is. Start by identifying a concern that frequently triggers your overthinking. Develop a clear, actionable plan to address this concern—outline the steps you need to take, identify the resources you require, and set a timeline for action. This approach not only diverts your mental energy from worrying to doing but also reinforces a sense of control and competence, which are natural antidotes to anxiety and insecurity.

Embracing these strategies not only alleviates the immediate distress caused by overthinking but also cultivates a more empowered and proactive mindset. As you learn to recognize, interrupt, and redirect patterns of overthinking, you regain control over your mental landscape, transforming it from a maze of worries into a garden of possibilities. This shift is not just about reducing anxiety but about enhancing your overall quality of life, where each thought contributes to building a reality defined by hope, action, and growth.

We've explored how mindfulness can anchor you in the present, strategies for identifying and managing emotional triggers, techniques for immediate emotional relief, and ways to cultivate deeper emotional resilience. Each of these segments provides you with tools not just for coping but for thriving amidst the complexities of relationships and personal challenges.

Chapter 5

Effective Communication Strategies

In the ever-changing tapestry of human relationships, communication is the thread that connects individuals together, creating patterns of understanding, trust, and connection. Yet, for someone navigating the complexities of an anxious attachment style, this thread can sometimes feel frayed or tangled. The fear of not being understood or of being too needy can mute your voice, leaving you feeling isolated within your own experiences. This chapter is dedicated to refining and strengthening your communication skills, transforming how you express yourself and connect with others, and enhancing the overall health of your relationships.

Assertive Communication: Expressing Your Needs

Understanding Assertiveness

At the heart of healthy interactions lies assertive communication—the balanced middle ground where your needs meet those of others with clarity and respect. Assertiveness is often misunderstood as aggression, but in reality, it is far from it. Being assertive means communicating your thoughts, feelings, and needs in a straightforward and respectful way without being passive or aggressive. It is about respecting your own rights and the rights of others. For someone with an anxious attachment style, mastering assertiveness can be particularly empowering. It allows you to articulate your needs and boundaries clearly, reducing the chances of misunderstandings and resentment, which can so often escalate anxieties and insecurities.

Assertive communication fosters self-respect and respect for others. It builds a foundation for relationships that thrive on honesty and mutual respect. This style of communication is especially crucial in moments when your insecurities might urge you to either withdraw (acting passively) or demand reassurance in a way that might overwhelm your partner (acting aggressively). By choosing assertiveness, you navigate a path that neither silences your needs nor imposes them forcefully upon others.

Expressing Needs Clearly

One of the most significant challenges you might face is the fear that expressing your needs will push others away—a common concern for those with an anxious attachment style. Here, clarity becomes your ally. Begin by identifying what you genuinely need from your relationships. Do you need more frequent communication, specific types of reassurance, or perhaps more quality time together? Once you have clarity about what you need, the next step is learning how to express these needs in a clear, concise, and calm manner.

When articulating your needs, use "I" statements. For example, instead of saying, "You don't spend enough time with me," you could say, "I feel valued when we spend quality time together. Could we plan a date night every week?" This approach expresses your feelings and requests without blaming or criticizing the other person, thereby reducing the likelihood of defensive responses.

Boundary Setting

An integral part of assertive communication involves setting and maintaining personal boundaries. Boundaries are the guidelines you set to protect your emotional well-being. They are not tools for controlling others but guidelines that help you respect yourself and teach others how to treat you. For you, setting boundaries might mean deciding not to respond to work emails at home or expressing that you need a certain amount of alone time each week for your hobbies.

In relationships, clearly communicating these boundaries is crucial. It involves being upfront about what you are comfortable with and what you are not. This clarity helps prevent feelings of resentment and exhaustion that can arise from overstepping personal limits. Remember, setting boundaries is not something you only do once; it is an ongoing process of understanding and asserting your needs as they evolve.

Practice Scenarios

To build your skill in assertive communication, consider engaging in practice scenarios either alone, with a therapist, or with a trusted friend. For example, you might role-play a situation where you need to express a boundary about how often you feel comfortable going out each week. Or, you might practice asking for a change in communication patterns with a partner.

Here's a simple template to guide your practice:

1. Identify the situation: Clearly state the context or issue.
2. Express your feelings: Use an "I" statement to express how you feel about the situation.
3. State your need: Clearly describe what you need or expect.

4. Request feedback: Ask the other person for their perspective or alternative solutions.

These practice scenarios can prepare you for real-life interactions, making it easier to navigate conversations with confidence and clarity.

By embracing assertive communication, you not only enhance your ability to express your needs and boundaries but also deepen your connections with others. This style of communication encourages a respectful, empathetic dialogue where both parties feel heard and valued. It's a step toward transforming the quality of your interactions and, ultimately, the quality of your relationships. As you continue to practice and integrate assertiveness into your daily interactions, you may find that the thread of communication not only holds strong but also enriches the tapestry of your relationships with vibrant patterns of mutual understanding and respect.

Listening Skills: The Key to Understanding

In the symphony of communication, where words are notes and silence is the rhythm, listening is not merely hearing the music but understanding its melody and meaning. For someone with an anxious attachment style, mastering the art of listening can be transformative. It's about tuning into not just the words being spoken but also the emotions and intentions behind them. This deeper understanding can alleviate fears of miscommunication and feelings of being misunderstood, which are often pervasive in anxious attachments.

Active Listening

Active listening is a skill that requires your full engagement and presence. It involves more than just hearing the words; it's about actively participating in the conversation by paying attention, showing that you're listening, providing feedback, and withholding judgment and advice. When you listen actively, you give the speaker a sense of worth and validation, showing that their thoughts and feelings matter to you. This can be particularly powerful in relationships where anxious thoughts often lead to misunderstandings.

To practice active listening, start by focusing entirely on the speaker. Avoid the temptation to think about how you're going to respond or what you're going to say next. Instead, focus on understanding their perspective. Show that you're listening by nodding, making eye contact, or using small verbal comments like "yes" or "I see." When they finish, reflect back on what you've heard to confirm your understanding, and ask clarifying questions if necessary. This process not only helps you grasp the full meaning of what's being discussed but also shows the speaker that they have your complete attention and respect.

Empathetic Listening

While active listening focuses on the 'how' of listening, empathetic listening delves deeper into the 'why' behind the speaker's words. It's about connecting with the speaker's emotions and understanding the situation from their perspective. Empathy in listening builds emotional bridges; it allows you to feel with the speaker, not just understand them intellectually. This form of listening can be particularly healing in relationships affected by anxious attachment, as it helps build a deep sense of emotional connection and trust.

To develop empathetic listening, try to tune into the emotions behind the speaker's words. What feelings are they expressing through their tone, pace, and choice of words? Reflect on how you would feel in their situation, which can help you connect more deeply with their emotional state. Respond in a way that acknowledges these emotions. For instance, if someone is expressing frustration, you might say, "It sounds like you're really overwhelmed by this situation." Such responses validate the speaker's feelings and can be incredibly affirming, especially for someone who struggles with feeling seen or heard in relationships.

Barriers to Effective Listening

Despite the best intentions, several barriers can impede effective listening. Common obstacles include distractions, preconceptions, and emotional reactivity. In today's digital age, distractions are more prevalent than ever; smartphones, computers, and various forms of media can pull your attention away from the crucial task of listening. To combat this, make a conscious effort to eliminate distractions when engaging in meaningful conversations. Turn off or put away electronic devices, and find a quiet space where you can focus entirely on the conversation.

Preconceptions and biases can also distort your listening. You might enter a conversation with pre-formed opinions about what the other person is going to say, which can prevent you from hearing their actual words and intentions. Challenge yourself to enter conversations with an open mind, setting aside your judgments to truly hear the other person. Lastly, emotional reactivity can hinder effective listening, especially if the conversation triggers anxiety or defensive reactions. When you notice yourself becoming emotionally reactive, take a few deep breaths to center yourself and remind yourself of the goal to understand, not to react.

Exercises to Improve Listening

To enhance your listening skills, consider engaging in exercises designed to refine your ability to listen attentively and empathetically. One effective exercise is the partner storytelling practice. Pair up with someone and take turns sharing a meaningful or challenging experience. While one person speaks, the other practices active and empathetic listening using the techniques discussed above. After the story, the listener should summarize what they heard and reflect back on the emotions they perceived, asking for confirmation to ensure accuracy. This exercise not only improves listening skills but also deepens mutual understanding and connection.

Another exercise involves listening to a speech or talking alone and then writing a summary of the key points and emotions conveyed. This practice can help sharpen your ability to distill information and tune into emotional undercurrents, which are crucial components of effective listening. Through these exercises and a committed approach to understanding and empathizing, you can transform how you listen, thereby enriching your relationships and easing the anxieties that often arise from miscommunications and misunderstandings. As you continue to practice and integrate these listening skills, you'll find that not only do your relationships improve, but so does your overall sense of connection and emotional fulfillment.

Navigating Difficult Conversations with Grace

Navigating difficult conversations is akin to walking through a delicate garden of thorns and blossoms—it requires careful steps, a keen awareness of your surroundings, and a gentle touch. Such conversations, whether they involve addressing grievances, discussing sensitive topics, or expressing deep-seated concerns, can stir a whirlpool of emotions, particularly for someone with an anxious attachment style. The anticipation of potential conflict can provoke anxiety, fear, and a multitude of scenarios playing out in your mind, each colored by past experiences and future worries. However, with the proper preparation and mindset, these conversations can transform from feared encounters into opportunities for growth and deeper connection.

Preparing for Difficult Conversations

Preparation is your first ally in transforming how you approach difficult conversations. This preparation involves not just thinking about what you want to say but also grounding yourself emotionally and mentally. Begin by reflecting on your objective for the conversation—what do you hope to achieve? Are you seeking to resolve a misunderstanding, change a behavior, or express a need? Clarifying your goals can help steer the conversation and prevent it from derailing into unproductive territories.

It's equally important to prepare emotionally by setting yourself in a state of calm and openness. Techniques such as deep breathing, meditation, or visualizing a successful conversation can be incredibly helpful. Visualize yourself expressing your thoughts clearly and receiving a responsive and considerate reaction. This mental practice can help build your confidence and reduce anxiety, setting a positive tone before the conversation even begins. Additionally, consider the timing and setting of the conversation—choose a moment and place free from distractions and conducive to privacy and calm. This shows respect not only for the process but also for the other person's comfort and readiness to engage in the discussion.

Maintaining Composure

Once in the conversation, maintaining composure is key to ensuring the discussion remains respectful and constructive. It's natural to feel emotional, but letting these emotions drive the conversation can lead to heightened tensions and conflict. One technique to maintain composure is mindful listening, which involves focusing fully on the other person's words without planning your rebuttal or response while they are speaking. This can help you understand their point of view and respond thoughtfully rather than impulsively.

Another strategy is to check in with your emotional state during the conversation regularly. If you feel your stress levels rising or emotions getting the better of you, don't hesitate to ask for a brief pause. A simple "Can we take a moment? I need to gather my thoughts" can give you time to breathe deeply, re-center yourself, and approach the conversation from a calmer perspective. Keeping your language clear, using "I" statements, and avoiding absolutes like "always" or "never" can also help maintain a constructive dialogue that is less likely to provoke defensive responses.

Conflict Resolution Skills

Practical conflict resolution skills are crucial in navigating difficult conversations successfully. One fundamental skill is the ability to identify and articulate both your needs and the other person's needs. Recognizing that both sets of needs are valid and important can foster empathy and understanding. From this understanding, you can explore solutions that accommodate both parties, which might involve compromise or finding a creative third option that neither of you had considered before.

Another essential conflict resolution technique is to keep the conversation focused on specific issues rather than generalizing or bringing up past conflicts. Focus on the present situation and seek to understand what can be done to resolve it. Ask open-ended questions to encourage healthy conversations and try to understand the other person's viewpoint. Phrases like "What do you feel would be the best way forward?" or "How can we improve this situation together?" can open up the conversation for collaborative problem-solving.

After the Conversation

Following a difficult conversation, it is essential to take time for personal reflection and relationship care. Reflect on what went well, what could have been improved, and what you learned about yourself and the other person. This reflection is a powerful tool for personal growth and honing your understanding of your relationship dynamics.

Additionally, show appreciation for the other person's willingness to engage in the conversation. A simple thank you can go a long way in reinforcing respect and appreciation between you both. If the conversation was particularly intense, consider engaging in a light, bonding activity together to restore positivity and comfort in the relationship. This could be something as simple as sharing a meal, watching a favorite show, or taking a walk together.

Navigating difficult conversations with grace involves preparation, presence, and a deep commitment to mutual understanding and respect. By approaching these conversations with the right tools and mindset, you transform potential conflicts into opportunities for strengthening trust and deepening connections, paving the way for more honest and supportive interactions in all areas of your life. As you continue to practice and refine these skills, you'll find that not only do your relationships benefit, but you also develop greater confidence and competence in handling whatever conversational challenges may come your way.

Feedback vs. Criticism: How to Tell the Difference

In the nuances of human interaction, especially when navigating relationships with a preoccupied and anxious attachment style, distinguishing between feedback and criticism can often feel like trying to find your way through a fog. Everything seems obscured and slightly out of reach. Understanding this distinction, however, is crucial as it not only affects how you perceive others' responses but also influences your emotional reactions and self-esteem. Feedback, ideally, is like a gentle hand guiding you back on track, meant to improve and encourage growth. Criticism, on the other hand, can feel like a push that sends you stumbling, often laden with judgment and not necessarily intended to foster improvement.

Identifying Feedback and Criticism

The first step in navigating the delicate waters of interpersonal feedback is to develop the ability to differentiate between constructive feedback and harmful criticism. Constructive feedback is typically specific, actionable, and focused on improvement. It is often delivered with a sense of respect and a desire to see positive outcomes. For example, if a partner says, "I feel loved when we talk about our days. Could we try to do that more often?" it provides a clear avenue for strengthening the relationship. This kind of feedback focuses on behaviors and actions, not on personal traits, which helps in maintaining self-esteem and promoting growth.

In contrast, criticism often lacks the constructive element and can be more about venting frustration or disappointment. It might target your character rather than your actions and lacks guidance on how to improve. An example could be, "You never listen to me," which not only generalizes behavior but also tags it as a personal failing without offering a solution or encouragement. This can trigger feelings of defensiveness and inadequacy, particularly if you're already sensitive to perceptions of rejection or not being good enough.

Receiving Feedback Gracefully

For someone with an anxious attachment style, receiving feedback, even when it's constructive, can sometimes feel like a critique of your worth. To handle feedback gracefully, start by reminding yourself that most feedback is not about undermining your value but about fostering personal or relational growth. When receiving feedback, try to listen actively—focus on the words being said without jumping to defend yourself or shutting down. Allow yourself a moment to process the information, separating any emotional surge from the content of the feedback.

A helpful approach is to ask clarifying questions. If your partner suggests wanting more communication, you might respond with, "What does ideal communication look like for you?" This shows your willingness to engage with the feedback without feeling attacked, and it turns the conversation into a collaborative discussion about improvement. It also helps you gather specific information that can guide your actions, making the feedback more valuable and less intimidating.

Giving Constructive Feedback

When it's your turn to give feedback, especially in a relationship colored by anxious attachment, the way you frame your words can make a significant difference. Start by focusing on your own feelings and experiences rather than on the other person's perceived faults. Use "I" statements to express how certain behaviors affect you, which can help prevent the other person from feeling attacked. For instance, saying, "I feel anxious when we don't talk about plans ahead of time. Could we start discussing our schedules more regularly?" directly communicates your needs without blaming the other person.

Be specific and clear about what changes you hope to see. Vague feedback can be confusing and hard to act upon, which might lead to frustration on both ends. Moreover, acknowledge the positive alongside the negative. This not only makes the feedback easier to receive but also reinforces the behaviors you appreciate, making it more likely that they will continue.

Dealing with Criticism

Despite your best efforts, there will be times when you face criticism, either constructive or otherwise, that hits hard emotionally. Dealing with criticism without letting it impact your self-esteem or your relationship involves several steps. First, allow yourself a moment to breathe and assess whether the criticism has any merit. If it does, consider what parts of it you can use to foster your growth. If it doesn't, try to let it go without internalizing the negativity.

It can also be helpful to discuss how you prefer to receive feedback with your partner or friends. Explaining that you respond best to specific, actionable comments rather than generalizations can guide how they provide feedback in the future, making it a constructive tool rather than a source of stress.

Navigating the delicate balance of giving and receiving feedback and criticism is a continual learning process. By fostering an environment where constructive feedback is the norm and criticism is handled with grace, you not only enhance your personal growth but also deepen your relationships, creating a safe space where emotional honesty leads to mutual betterment rather than distress. As you practice these skills, remember that each conversation is an opportunity to refine your communication, ensuring that every word spoken or heard serves to strengthen, not strain, the connections you cherish.

Resolving Conflicts without Losing Yourself

In the complex dance of relationships, conflicts are bound to happen. They arise from differences in opinion, desires, and expectations. For someone with a preoccupied attachment style, these conflicts can often feel like threats, not just to the relationship but to your own emotional safety. It is crucial, then, to approach conflict resolution not just as a means to resolve disagreements but as an opportunity to affirm your values and preserve your sense of self. This delicate balance needs a deep understanding of how to stay true to yourself, negotiate effectively, avoid power struggles, and maintain the overall health of the relationship.

Staying True to Yourself

Amidst the give-and-take of resolving disagreements, it's essential to remain anchored to your core values and identity. This alignment ensures that the compromises you make do not come at the cost of losing yourself or your values. Begin by clearly understanding what is non-negotiable for you—these are usually aspects tied closely to your values and ethics. For instance, if honesty and loyalty are values you hold dear, any resolution that requires you to compromise these may leave you feeling dissatisfied and disconnected from your true self.

Communicating your values clearly to your partner is just as important as understanding them yourself. This clarity helps set the boundaries for what compromises are acceptable and what aren't. It also invites your partner to understand and respect where you're coming from, which can foster a deeper mutual respect. Approaching conflict with this level of authenticity encourages a resolution that respects both partners' true selves, facilitating a solution that enhances the relationship without diminishing either person.

Negotiation and Compromise

Finding a resolution that satisfies both parties often involves negotiation and compromise—a process where open communication and mutual respect are paramount. Start by expressing your perspective and needs clearly, employing the assertive communication skills discussed earlier. Then, equally important, invite your partner to share their views and needs.

The key to effective negotiation lies in looking for solutions that meet the underlying needs of both partners, not just surface wants. For example, if you and your partner are arguing about spending habits, rather than digging in your heels about specific expenditures, try to understand what each of you values about money—security, enjoyment, freedom, or stability. With this understanding, you can look for financial plans that respect these values rather than just one person's spending desires.

Compromise does not mean one person giving in to the other's demands; instead, it's about finding a middle ground where both can feel satisfied with the outcome. Sometimes, this might mean taking turns giving and taking or finding a completely new solution that neither of us had considered before. The willingness to bend but not break is crucial in finding compromises that uphold the integrity of the relationship while also honoring individual needs and desires.

Avoiding Power Struggles

Power struggles arise when conflicts shift from trying to resolve an issue to trying to win an argument. These struggles can escalate disputes, leading to resentment and a breakdown in communication. To avoid this, focus on the issue at hand rather than on asserting dominance or control. Recognize when the discussion shifts from constructive problem-solving to a battle of wills. At this point, it might be helpful to take a step back, perhaps even taking a break from the discussion to cool down and refocus on what you are both trying to achieve.

Maintaining a posture of collaboration rather than competition is critical. Remind yourself and your partner that you are on the same team, aiming to strengthen your relationship rather than 'win' an argument. This mindset can help keep power dynamics in check, promoting a healthier, more equal approach to conflict resolution.

Maintaining Relationship Health

Ultimately, the goal of conflict resolution should be to enhance the relationship, making it stronger, more resilient, and more understanding. This means the focus should not only be on resolving the immediate conflict but also on fostering the long-term health of the relationship. Regularly invest in the relationship by spending quality time together, communicating openly about each other's needs and desires, and showing appreciation for one another. These practices can build a strong foundation that can withstand the pressures of conflict when they arise.

Moreover, after resolving a conflict, take the time to reconnect with your partner. Engage in activities that both of you enjoy, offer words of affirmation, or simply spend some quiet time together. These moments can heal any residual stress from the conflict, reinforcing your bond and reminding you both of the love and respect that underlies your relationship.

Navigating conflicts isn't just about finding solutions but about growing together and deepening your understanding of each other. Each conflict, handled well, can be a stepping stone to a more mature, fulfilling relationship. As you move forward, remember that the strength of your bond is not measured by the absence of conflicts but by how you choose to address and resolve them together.

These tools are not just mechanisms for dealing with disagreements but are essential components of building a loving, resilient partnership. In the next chapter, we will explore healthy dating practices, further enhancing your ability to forge meaningful and fulfilling connections.

Chapter 6

Healthy Dating Practices for the Anxiously Attached

Dating and meeting new people is like stepping into a garden where each path promises a new adventure, and every turn offers a chance to discover something incredible. Yet, each step is tinged with a whisper of uncertainty that stirs the leaves around you. Such is the world of dating, especially when navigated with an anxious attachment style. This chapter aims to transform that whisper of uncertainty into a song of self-assurance, guiding you through the digital landscapes of dating apps where opportunities for connection are vast and the potential for personal growth is immense.

Navigating Dating Apps Without Anxiety

Choosing the Right Platform

The first step in cultivating a positive online dating experience is selecting a platform that aligns with your relationship goals and personal comfort level. Each dating app has its own culture and norms, some fostering quick, surface-level interactions, while others promote deeper connections. Think about what you are truly looking for: Are you interested in a long-term partnership, or are you exploring different types of relationships? Platforms like eHarmony or Match might be suited for those seeking long-term commitments, given their algorithms and profiles that focus on compatibility in significant areas like values, lifestyle, and interests. In contrast, apps like Tinder or Bumble offer a more flexible approach, which can be ideal if you're exploring or if you prefer more control over who you can connect with. Take your time to research and try different platforms. Consider starting with a free version to get a feel for the app's interface and user base before committing to a paid subscription, which often offers more features and connectivity.

Setting Healthy Expectations

Setting realistic expectations is crucial in mitigating anxiety when using dating apps. It's easy to get swept up in the possibilities, imagining each swipe or message as a step closer to your ideal relationship. However, this perspective can lead to disappointment if interactions don't meet your hoped-for outcomes. To set healthy expectations, remind yourself that dating is a process of exploration. Each interaction is an opportunity to learn more about your preferences, communication styles, and what you truly desire in a relationship. Not every person you match with will lead to a deep connection, and that's okay. Treat each conversation as a learning experience, not a test of your worth or desirability.

Protecting Emotional Well-being

Engaging in online dating requires attention to your emotional health, particularly when you navigate these waters with an anxious attachment style. It's essential to stay attuned to your feelings and recognize when you might be overextending yourself emotionally. Implement boundaries around how much time you spend on dating apps. Excessive swiping or constant messaging can lead to burnout and increase anxiety, making it hard to remain centered and enjoy the process. Consider setting specific times for app interaction, perhaps an hour each evening, allowing you to engage fully in the experience without it overwhelming your day or impacting your mental health negatively.

Communication Tips

Effective communication on dating platforms is crucial in establishing meaningful connections. Start by being honest and authentic in your profile and your messages. This doesn't mean sharing every detail of your life immediately but rather showing your true self in your interests, your humor, and what you're looking for in a partner. When messaging, ask open-ended questions that invite more than a yes-or-no answer, such as "What inspired you to pick up a guitar?" over "Do you like music?" These types of questions can lead to deeper conversations and help you gauge the compatibility between you and your match.

The way you communicate can also set the tone for future interactions. If anxiety makes you prone to rush text responses or overanalyze messages, take a moment to breathe and compose your thoughts. Remember, each exchange is just one small step in the broader journey of getting to know someone—there's no need to rush or force a connection.

Reflection Section

Reflect on your current approach to online dating with these prompts:

- What aspects of online dating do you find most anxiety-provoking?
- How do your interactions on dating apps reflect your attachment style?

- What boundaries might you set to protect your emotional well-being while dating online?

Use these reflections to adjust your approach, ensuring that your online dating experience is healthy, enjoyable, and true to who you are. By understanding and integrating these practices, you empower yourself not just to navigate the complexities of dating apps but to thrive within them, turning each swipe into a stroke of self-discovery and each match into a melody of possibility.

The Dos and Don'ts of Early Dating Stages

Venturing into the early stages of a new relationship can feel like navigating a delicate maze where each step reflects your hopes and vulnerabilities. Understanding how to maintain your boundaries, pace the development of the relationship, and stay present can significantly influence the health and potential longevity of this new connection. Let's explore these concepts to ensure that as you lay the foundation of a new relationship, it is both sturdy and nurturing.

Maintaining Boundaries

One of the most vital aspects to establish from the onset of any relationship is a clear set of personal boundaries. These are not just about safeguarding your well-being but also about nurturing mutual respect and understanding between you and your partner. A boundary might be as simple as how often you are comfortable communicating or as complex as setting limits on emotional and physical intimacy until you feel more secure in the relationship. It's essential to communicate these boundaries clearly and assertively—not as demands, but as necessary guidelines for ensuring your comfort and emotional safety.

Moreover, while it's crucial to set boundaries, it's equally important to respect and understand the boundaries set by your partner. This reciprocal respect for boundaries not only prevents potential conflicts but also deepens trust, creating a safe space where both you and your partner feel valued and understood. Remember, boundaries are not static; they can evolve as the relationship grows and as you both become more comfortable with each other. Regular check-ins about what's working and what isn't can help adjust boundaries as needed, ensuring they always reflect your current comfort levels and emotional needs.

Avoiding Common Pitfalls

In the whirlwind of new relationships, particularly for those with an anxious attachment style, it's easy to fall into certain pitfalls that can amplify anxieties and insecurities. One common pitfall is the tendency to idealize the partner or the relationship too quickly. While it's natural to be excited and optimistic, placing your partner or the relationship on a pedestal can create unrealistic expectations that lead to disappointment and increased anxiety when they are inevitably unmet. Instead, try to see the relationship and the person you are dating as they are, not through a lens of what you hope or imagine them to be.

Another pitfall is overdependence, where the emotional or even social reliance on a new partner becomes overwhelming. This overdependence can stifle the natural development of the relationship and lead to a dynamic where your self-worth and happiness are too closely tied to your partner's presence and reassurance. To avoid this, continue to nurture your hobbies, friendships, and responsibilities. They will not only keep you grounded and balanced but also enrich your personal growth and contribute to a healthier relationship.

Pacing the Relationship

The speed at which a relationship develops can significantly impact its success and durability. Particularly when feelings are intense, there's a temptation to rush through relationship milestones in an attempt to secure commitment and alleviate underlying anxieties about abandonment or rejection. However, rushing can prevent you from fully understanding your feelings and assessing compatibility.

Taking the time to let the relationship naturally unfold allows you to gather insights into your mutual compatibility, values, and goals. It helps in building a solid foundation based on genuine understanding and appreciation rather than on the anxious rush to alleviate insecurities. Communicate openly with your partner about your ideal pace and try to find a rhythm that respects both of your needs. This conversation itself can deepen your connection and ensure that both of you feel comfortable with how the relationship is progressing.

Mindful Dating

Finally, embracing a mindful approach to dating can transform your experience from one of anxiety to one of enjoyment and meaningful connection. Mindful dating involves being present in each moment with your partner without overly focusing on past experiences or future possibilities. It encourages an appreciation of the current experience—whether it's a conversation, an activity, or a quiet moment together.

Practicing mindfulness helps you process and enjoy each stage of your relationship without the typical anxieties about where it is heading. It allows you to form a connection based on true togetherness and shared experiences rather than on the anxieties driven by attachment fears. Simple practices like focusing on your breath during dates, actively listening to your partner, and expressing gratitude for the time spent together can enhance your ability to stay present and deeply connected.

By embracing these principles in the early stages of dating, you create a robust framework for a fulfilling, respectful, and non-toxic relationship. This approach not only supports your emotional health but also sets a precedent for future interactions and developments within the relationship, fostering a genuine, stable, and deeply connected bond.

Recognizing Red Flags and Deal Breakers

In the delicate dance of beginning a new relationship, it's crucial to be vigilant about the signs and signals that may indicate potential problems down the road. These are often referred to as red flags—certain behaviors or patterns that, if ignored, can evolve into significant issues, potentially derailing a healthy relationship. Recognizing these early warning signs is akin to reading the weather before setting sail; it equips you with the knowledge to navigate or, if necessary, change course to avoid a storm.

The process of identifying red flags is fundamentally about observation and intuition. For instance, consistently dismissive or disrespectful behavior towards others, inability to respect your boundaries, or an evident lack of communication skills are all red flags. These behaviors might initially seem minor or easy to dismiss, especially when you are attracted to the person or excited about the new relationship. However, they can be a sign of deeper issues that could affect your emotional well-being and relationship satisfaction in the long term. Pay attention to how your date treats service staff, interacts with family, or talks about past relationships. Patterns of behavior that include blaming others excessively can be a warning sign of how they might eventually treat you.

Understanding your personal deal breakers is equally vital. These are the traits or behaviors that you consider non-negotiable in a relationship, and they often stem from your core values and relationship goals. For example, if honesty is a core value for you, then deceitful behavior may be a deal breaker. If you highly value independence, then someone who shows co-dependent tendencies might not be the right match for you. Clarifying your deal breakers involves a deep dive into your values and requires you to be honest with yourself about what you truly need in a relationship to feel fulfilled and secure. This clarity can prevent you from getting mixed up in relationships that are doomed from the start because they fundamentally conflict with your values or needs.

Trusting your intuition plays a critical role in this process. Intuition is that gut feeling that something is off, even if you can't immediately put your finger on why. It's an invaluable tool in the early stages of dating, helping you discern subtleties in behavior that may not align with what you're seeking in a partner. However, for those with an anxious attachment style, distinguishing between intuition and anxiety can be challenging. Anxiety often paints scenarios based on fear rather than reality, while intuition is a quieter, more subtle sense of knowing. Practicing mindfulness can help you listen to your intuition more effectively by calming the mind and reducing anxiety, thereby allowing your inner voice to come through more clearly.

When red flags are evident, addressing them constructively and respectfully is crucial. This doesn't necessarily mean ending the relationship immediately but rather engaging in open and honest communication about your concerns. Approach the conversation with a focus on your feelings and perceptions, using "I" statements to avoid putting the other person on the defensive. For example, saying, "I felt uncomfortable when you interrupted me multiple times during dinner; I value being listened to," directly addresses the behavior without making broad character judgments. This approach allows space for the person to understand your perspective and, ideally, discuss ways to adjust their behavior.

Navigating early dating stages with an awareness of red flags and deal breakers, trusting your intuition, and addressing concerns openly sets a foundation for healthier and more fulfilling relationships. It empowers you to steer clear of potential heartache and invest your time and energy in relationships that genuinely align with your values and life goals. As you continue to apply these lessons, remember that each interaction is a chance to grow, bringing you closer to the relationship you desire and deserve.

Setting Healthy Pace and Boundaries in New Relationships

In the delicate beginnings of a relationship, understanding and establishing a pace that feels comfortable for both you and your partner is akin to cultivating a garden—it requires mindfulness about when to plant seeds and how often to water them to ensure they grow into healthy plants. The speed at which a relationship evolves can have a deep impact on its health and longevity. Rushing might lead to overlooking fundamental mismatches in values or compatibility while moving too slowly could stem from fear and inhibit genuine connection. Recognizing the importance of timing helps in nurturing a relationship that can thrive.

Timing in relationships often relates to how quickly you and your partner move through different stages—from dating to becoming exclusive, meeting friends and family, or cohabitating. Each step should ideally feel like a natural progression, not a hurried leap or a hesitant shuffle. It's essential to frequently check in with yourself and communicate openly with your partner about where you feel the relationship is heading. If you ever feel pressured to speed things up or slow them down, it might be a signal to reassess not only the relationship's pace but also the reasons behind these feelings. Perhaps anxiety is pushing you to rush into a commitment to secure reassurance, or fear of getting hurt is causing you to hold back. Reflecting on these motivations allows you to address underlying issues and adjust the relationship's pace to one that fosters security and happiness for both parties.

The art of communicating personal boundaries ties directly into the pacing of a new relationship. Boundaries are your personal guidelines, rules, or limits that identify reasonable and permissible ways for others to behave towards you. Clearly articulating your boundaries involves self-awareness and courage, especially if you fear that setting them might drive the other person away. However, expressing your boundaries is about honoring your needs and ensuring that the relationship respects your values and space. For instance, if you are not ready to discuss past relationships, stating this boundary clearly helps your partner understand your current needs and respects your emotional space. Effective communication about boundaries not only helps avoid feelings of resentment or discomfort but also deepens mutual respect and understanding.

Respecting your partner's boundaries is just as crucial as setting your own. When your partner communicates their limits, listen attentively, seek to understand their perspective, and adjust your behavior accordingly. This mutual respect for boundaries prevents overstepping and the potential emotional fallout that can follow. It also sets a foundation of trust and safety that is crucial for any relationship to prosper. If you find it challenging to accept or understand a boundary set by your partner, discuss it openly. Perhaps you need more clarity on why a particular boundary is essential to them or how you can support them in maintaining it. This open dialogue can prevent misunderstandings and ensure that both partners feel valued and respected.

Lastly, the willingness to adjust the pace of a relationship is a testament to its resilience. Relationships are dynamic—what works one month might not work the next. Life events, personal growth, or changes in emotional needs can all influence how a relationship should progress. Maintaining flexibility in how you and your partner navigate these changes is crucial. For example, suppose one partner experiences a stressful period at work. In that case, the other might need to be more patient and supportive, temporarily adjusting expectations for time spent together or emotional availability. This adaptability not only helps the relationship endure through challenging times but also strengthens the bond between partners, as it is built on a deep understanding and respect for each other's evolving needs.

Navigating the pace of a relationship and maintaining healthy boundaries requires a delicate balance of communication, respect, and flexibility. By continually engaging with these practices, you ensure that the relationship grows at a pace that is comfortable and fulfilling for both you and your partner, fostering a robust, respectful, and deeply connected partnership.

The Importance of Maintaining Individuality in Early Dating

When you enter the fresh and exciting phase of a new relationship, it's like stepping into a new landscape filled with the potential for discovery and adventure. However, amidst this excitement, maintaining a strong and distinct sense of self is crucial. The thrill of a new romance can sometimes sweep you away, tempting you to merge your identity with that of your partner. This merging might feel right in the rush of new love, but preserving your individuality is important to the long-term health and happiness of both your personal development and the relationship.

Preserving Self-Identity

Keeping a robust sense of self in a new relationship involves consciously engaging in activities and practices that reflect your personal values and interests. It's important to continue investing time in hobbies and activities that you love outside of those you share with your partner. This not only nurtures your soul but also keeps your identity diversified and grounded. For instance, if you're passionate about painting or playing an instrument, set aside regular time each week to indulge in these pursuits. This commitment reinforces your identity as an individual, not just as a partner, and brings a richer, more varied energy back into your relationship. Additionally, maintaining strong connections with friends and family can provide emotional support and a sense of continuity and grounding, reminding you of your life's narrative before your romantic relationship began.

Balancing Interests

The art of balancing personal interests with the desire to spend time with your new partner can be likened to weaving: you aim to create a beautiful tapestry of shared and individual experiences. It involves negotiating time and energy, ensuring that neither your personal interests nor the relationship are neglected. This balance might mean sometimes inviting your partner to join in your hobbies while at other times partaking in theirs. However, it is equally important to have pursuits that you keep just for yourself, as they fortify your independence and self-expression. Open communication about how you value your personal passions can help your partner understand and respect your need for this balance, potentially leading to a deeper appreciation of each other as whole, multifaceted individuals.

Avoiding Over-Identification

Over-identification with your partner or the relationship happens when your self-esteem and self-worth begin to depend heavily on your relationship status or partner's approval. This dependency can cloud your judgment, compromise your decision-making, and lead to a loss of self. To avoid this, it's vital to engage in regular self-reflection. Reflect on how your decisions are made within the relationship—are they in alignment with your true self, or are they overly influenced by a desire to please your partner or secure their affection? Keeping a journal is a useful way to check in with yourself and make sure that your actions and choices reflect your true feelings and values rather than an over-identification with your relationship.

Independent Growth

Encouraging personal growth independent of your relationship is essential. This growth can involve developing new skills, advancing in your career, or pursuing personal projects. These achievements contribute to your self-esteem and personal fulfillment, which are foundational to a healthy relationship. When both partners are growing and evolving independently, their relationship is likely to be dynamic and resilient, capable of thriving through change. Moreover, this independent growth fosters mutual respect and admiration between partners, as each person brings new insights, experiences, and energies into the relationship, keeping it vibrant and enriching.

In essence, while new relationships are exhilarating and fulfilling, they also require you to consciously maintain your individuality and personal growth. This balance isn't always easy, but it is profoundly rewarding. As you continue to cultivate your personal interests, balance your time, and encourage independent growth, not only do you enhance your own life, but you also bring a richer, more whole self to your relationship, creating a dynamic where both partners thrive individually and together.

Remember the importance of nurturing your individuality even as you grow closer to someone new. The strategies discussed here are not just about maintaining a sense of self but are crucial for building a sustaining relationship. In the next chapter, we will explore more profound aspects of relationship dynamics, focusing on long-term relationship success and how to continue nurturing a healthy, loving connection as your relationship evolves.

Chapter 7

Long-Term Relationship Success

Every relationship requires continuous nurturing to maintain its health and vibrancy. This chapter is dedicated to exploring how you can keep the love alive, making sure that your relationship not only survives but thrives in the long term.

Keeping Love Alive: Relationship Nurturing Techniques

Continuous Engagement

Keeping a relationship dynamic and engaging over the years can sometimes feel like trying to keep a flame alive in a gust of wind. It's easy to slip into routine and complacency, which can slowly diminish the vibrant connection that once sparked between you and your partner. To combat this, it's crucial to inject new life into your interactions regularly. This might mean setting aside time each week to try something new together, be it a cooking class, exploring a part of town you've never visited, or simply dedicating an evening to share music from your youth or books you love. These activities not only break the monotony but also provide fresh content for conversation and shared experiences, which are the bedrock of continuous engagement.

Prioritizing Quality Time

Amidst the hustle of daily life—juggling careers, perhaps raising children, and managing a household—it can be challenging to carve out quality time for each other. However, the importance of this practice cannot be overstressed. Quality time is that undistracted, intentional time spent together that deepens your connection and reaffirms your commitment to each other. It might look like regular date nights, weekend getaways, or simply quiet evenings at home without the interference of technology or other distractions. It's these moments, when given full attention to each other, that you genuinely see and are seen by your partner, reinforcing the emotional bond that initially brought you together.

Maintaining Physical Connection

Physical intimacy is another pillar of a long-lasting relationship. It's not just about sex—although maintaining a healthy sexual relationship is crucial—it's also about daily physical connections like kissing, holding hands, and cuddling. These actions release oxytocin, often referred to as the 'love hormone,' which enhances a sense of closeness and well-being. Physical intimacy acts as a glue that holds the relationship together, providing comfort and pleasure. It's important to communicate openly about your physical needs and to be attentive to the changes that might occur in your and your partner's desires over time, addressing them with sensitivity and understanding.

Expressing Appreciation

In the dance of long-term relationships, the steps of gratitude and appreciation keep the rhythm smooth and enjoyable. It's easy to take each other for granted as time passes, but regularly expressing appreciation can significantly impact the health of your relationship. This doesn't only mean saying "thank you" for the big gestures, like planning a surprise birthday party or handling a major household repair. It's equally, if not more important, to acknowledge the everyday actions—making the bed, listening to you recount your day, or making you a cup of coffee in the morning. Verbal affirmations, leaving little notes, or even a quick text can make your partner feel valued and loved. Regularly expressing gratitude fosters a positive cycle where both partners feel more appreciated and motivated to keep contributing to the relationship's happiness.

Reflection Section

Take a moment to reflect on the nurturing techniques discussed:

- Which of these techniques do you currently practice regularly in your relationship?
- Are there new strategies you feel inspired to try?
- What simple action could you take today to enhance your connection with your partner?

Use these reflections to bring new insights and practices into your relationship, ensuring that it continues to grow and flourish. By actively engaging in these nurturing techniques, you not only maintain but also enrich the garden of your relationship, allowing it to thrive through every season of life.

Balancing Togetherness and Independence

Nurturing a relationship where both togetherness and independence coexist harmoniously is like walking a tightrope, balancing the shared weight of mutual desires with the personal aspirations of each individual. It needs a deep understanding and respect for the need to foster individual interests as well as the importance of experiencing life together. As someone with an anxious attachment style, you may find this balance particularly challenging, as the desire for closeness can sometimes overshadow the need for personal space and self-discovery. However, embracing this balance is not only crucial for your personal growth but also for the health of your relationship.

Fostering Individual Interests

Supporting each other when pursuing personal interests and hobbies might seem like a simple act, yet it is profound in its impact on a relationship. When partners are engaged in activities they are passionate about, separately from one another, it brings fresh energy and vitality back into the relationship. Each partner's pursuit of personal passions not only leads to individual fulfillment but also adds an intriguing layer of complexity and attractiveness to their persona. This dynamic allows each person to grow independently, bringing new ideas, experiences, and enthusiasm into the relationship, which can be incredibly revitalizing.

It is essential, however, to communicate openly about the time spent on individual activities to ensure it does not become a source of neglect or resentment within the relationship. Discuss how you can support each other's interests, perhaps by dedicating specific times for these activities, thus ensuring that while personal growth is prioritized, the relationship remains nurtured and valued. This support not only shows love and respect for each other's individuality but also strengthens the bond, as each partner feels genuinely seen and appreciated for who they are beyond the relationship.

Respecting Alone Time

The significance of respecting each other's need for alone time cannot be overstated, especially in long-term relationships where the lines between togetherness and individuality can sometimes blur. Alone time is a sacred space for self-reflection, relaxation, and personal growth. It allows each partner to decompress, process emotions, and maintain their sense of self. This practice is particularly beneficial for you, as it can help you deal with feelings of anxiety and dependence that often accompany anxious attachment styles.

Communicating the need for alone time without offending your partner or triggering their insecurities involves clear, compassionate dialogue. It's about expressing the need for space in a way that reassures your partner of your love and commitment while emphasizing the importance of this time for your personal well-being. For instance, explaining that time spent reading, meditating, or simply being alone helps you recharge and bring your best self to the relationship can help your partner understand and respect your need for space.

Joint Activities

While fostering individuality is key, selecting and engaging in activities that both partners enjoy is equally important. These mutual experiences are the threads that weave the fabric of your relationship, creating memories and bonds that can strengthen your connection. Whether it's hiking, cooking, traveling, or engaging in artistic pursuits together, these activities provide opportunities for joy, learning, and a deeper understanding of each other.

The key to success in shared activities lies in finding pursuits that resonate with both partners, allowing each person to engage fully and authentically. It's about compromise and exploration, discovering new shared interests that can evolve into meaningful traditions. Regularly scheduling time for these shared activities can help maintain the connection and ensure that both partners feel valued and engaged in the relationship.

Supporting Each Other's Goals

The essence of a supportive relationship lies not only in how you handle the present but also in how you support each other's visions for the future. Supporting each other's personal and professional goals is crucial in nurturing a relationship that is both fulfilling and forward-moving. This support can manifest in various ways, from being a sounding board for ideas to assisting in practical ways, such as taking on extra responsibilities at home when one partner is pursuing a degree or a demanding project at work.

This support not only strengthens the relationship by building a sense of partnership and teamwork but also deepens mutual respect and admiration. It demonstrates a commitment to each other's happiness and success, which can be incredibly affirming, especially for people with an anxious attachment style who may struggle with fears of abandonment or not being a priority. By actively supporting each other's goals, you reinforce the message that the relationship is not just about being together in the present but also about encouraging each other's growth and success in the long term.

In integrating these practices into your relationship, you create a dynamic where independence and togetherness are not at odds but are interwoven in a way that enhances personal fulfillment and relationship satisfaction. This balance is not always easy to achieve and requires ongoing effort, communication, and adjustment. However, the rewards of such a balanced approach are profound, leading to a relationship that is both secure and liberating, allowing both partners to thrive individually and as a couple.

Effective Coping Strategies for Relationship Anxiety

Anxiety in relationships is like a silent current that can subtly unsettle the waters between partners, sometimes without clear reason or warning. If you find yourself often caught in the ripples of relationship anxiety, knowing how to identify what triggers these feelings can be as empowering as learning to swim against the current. Each person's triggers are deeply personal, often rooted in past experiences or fears about the future. For you, it might be a delayed response to a text message or an offhand comment that seems to hint at disinterest. Being mindful of these triggers is the first step in managing your anxiety—not just acknowledging their existence but understanding their origins and the specific contexts in which they arise.

Developing this awareness requires a blend of self-reflection and acute observation. Pay attention to the moments when your anxiety peaks. What was said? What actions preceded it? How did you feel physically and emotionally? Keeping a journal can be particularly insightful here. Documenting your feelings and the situations that trigger them creates a record that can help you identify patterns and the often subtle nuances that signal the onset of anxiety. This understanding helps you anticipate and prepare for these feelings rather than being caught off-guard.

Communication as a Tool

Once you've identified your triggers, communication becomes an essential tool in managing relationship anxiety. This isn't just about expressing your feelings to your partner, though that is undoubtedly important, but also about creating an ongoing dialogue that addresses and reassesses anxieties as they evolve. Open and honest communication helps nurture a supportive relationship where vulnerabilities can be shared without fear of judgment. This involves discussing your triggers explicitly, explaining why certain behaviors or situations make you anxious, and what kind of responses from your partner might help alleviate these feelings.

Moreover, this communication should be a two-way street, where you are also receptive to hearing and understanding your partner's feelings and potential anxieties. Such exchanges can deepen mutual understanding and foster a supportive environment that mitigates the roots of anxiety. It's also helpful to set regular check-ins where both partners can honestly discuss their feelings and the health of the relationship. These conversations can reinforce security and stability, providing reassurance and a sense of shared commitment to overcoming challenges together.

Self-Soothing Techniques

While communication with your partner is crucial, developing strategies to manage anxiety independently is equally important. Self-soothing techniques are tools you can use to calm your mind and body, helping you regain balance and perspective. Deep breathing exercises, for example, can be incredibly effective. They help slow down your heart rate and reduce the intensity of anxiety symptoms, making it easier to think clearly. Practicing Techniques such as guided imagery, where you visualize a peaceful and safe place, can also provide a mental escape from stressful thoughts.

Seeking External Support

Sometimes, anxiety can feel too heavy to manage alone or even with the support of your partner. In such cases, seeking external support can be a wise and proactive step. Couples counseling, for example, offers a structured environment where you can explore the roots of your relationship anxiety with professional guidance. A therapist can help you and your partner develop new communication strategies, deeper understanding, and more effective ways to support each other.

Individual therapy can be helpful, especially if your anxiety stems from experiences or issues that predate your current relationship. A therapist can help you dissect these personal histories, providing tools and insights that are tailored to your specific needs and challenges. Additionally, support groups for those with anxious attachment styles can offer a sense of community and understanding, where you can learn from others' experiences while sharing your own.

Engaging with these external resources can reinforce your internal efforts, providing a comprehensive support system that empowers you to manage relationship anxiety more effectively. Whether through professional counseling, support groups, or a combination of both, seeking external support underscores a commitment to personal and relational health, paving the way for more stable and satisfying partnerships.

The Role of Shared Goals and Values in Long-term Stability

In the evolving narrative of a long-term relationship, the alignment of life goals between partners is not merely beneficial but essential for harmony and enduring connection. Imagine this alignment as the spine of a book, holding together various pages that, while individually unique, collectively tell a coherent and compelling story. When life goals are aligned—be they related to career aspirations, family planning, personal development, or lifestyle choices—it creates a unified direction that both partners travel together, each step reinforcing their bond and shared purpose. This doesn't mean you need to share identical goals, but there should be a significant overlap or, at the very least, a mutual support system for individual aspirations that respects the relationship's shared objectives.

For example, if one partner dreams of living abroad for a few years while the other values establishing deep roots near family, it's crucial to discuss these aspirations openly. Such conversations can lead to creative solutions that honor both desires, perhaps by compromising on a shorter-term stay abroad or planning frequent home visits. The key lies in viewing these discussions as opportunities for deeper understanding and mutual support rather than points of contention.

Navigating value differences presents its own unique set of challenges and opportunities within a relationship. Values deeply influence thoughts, actions, and reactions, and differences in this arena can lead to conflict if not handled with care and respect. However, these differences also offer rich soil for the growth and expansion of personal worldviews. When you encounter a difference in values, approach it with curiosity rather than judgment. Engage in open-ended conversations that explore why these values are important to each of you. Understanding the roots of each other's values fosters empathy and can often reveal underlying commonalities that might not be apparent at first glance.

For example, you may value career success because it provides a sense of achievement and security, while your partner might prioritize leisure and the freedom it brings. Rather than viewing these as conflicting, explore how both values contribute to a well-rounded life, promoting a balance between work and relaxation. This understanding can transform potential conflicts into a cohesive strategy that supports both partners' happiness and fulfillment.

The process of joint decision-making is another critical element that reinforces equality and partnership in a relationship. It involves making choices together on matters big and small, from deciding on weekend plans to choosing a home or making financial investments. This collaborative approach ensures that both voices are heard and valued, which is crucial for maintaining a sense of fairness and mutual respect. It also builds a framework of teamwork, reinforcing the notion that you are in this together, facing challenges and making decisions as a united front.

To facilitate effective joint decision-making, start by setting clear communication rules that ensure both partners can express their thoughts and feelings without interruption. Use techniques like reflective listening, where you repeat back what your partner has said to confirm understanding, which can help clarify communications and deepen mutual understanding. Additionally, be willing to compromise and sometimes accept decisions that might not be your first choice, recognizing that the health of the relationship can depend on flexibility and mutual concessions.

Finally, the necessity of periodically renegotiating goals and expectations as both partners grow and change cannot be overstated. Just as individuals evolve, so too does a relationship. What was important to you or worked for you five years ago might not hold the same significance now. Regularly checking in on your goals and expectations can prevent feelings of discontent or misalignment from festering under the surface. These check-ins can be structured, perhaps during an annual relationship review, or more informal, emerging naturally during shared quiet moments or over dinner conversations.

Consider using these times to discuss any new interests, aspirations, or changes in belief that might have developed. Openly discussing these changes can prevent surprises and ensure that the relationship adapts and grows in alignment with each partner's evolving self. This dynamic process not only respects the individual growth of each partner but also nurtures a relationship that is vibrant, responsive, and deeply connected to the current realities of both partners' lives.

By embracing these practices, you weave a relationship tapestry that is rich with shared goals, respectful of differences, and robust in its decision-making and adaptability. This approach not only fortifies the relationship against potential stresses but also enhances the joy and fulfillment derived from a partnership that truly understands and supports its members' evolving journeys.

Renewing Commitment: When Relationships Hit Rough Patches

In the life of every relationship, there will be moments that test the strength and resilience of the bond between partners. These rough patches, whether sparked by external stressors or internal conflicts, can seem daunting. However, with the right perspective, they also present invaluable opportunities for growth and deepening connections. It's in these times that the fabric of your relationship is stretched and tested, and with conscious effort, it can emerge even stronger and more intricate than before.

Recognizing Growth Opportunities

Every challenge that arises in your relationship holds the potential to teach you more about each other and yourselves, deepening your understanding and empathy. For instance, a disagreement over financial decisions can reveal underlying values and fears that may not have been previously discussed. Viewing these challenges as opportunities rather than setbacks can transform the way you interact with each other during these times. It encourages a mindset of curiosity and openness, where the focus changes from assigning blame to exploring solutions and learning from the experience. This approach not only alleviates the immediate tension but also builds a toolkit of emotional and communicative strategies that strengthen the relationship for future challenges.

Renewal Rituals

Creating rituals or milestones can play a pivotal role in renewing and reaffirming your commitment to each other. These rituals can be as simple as an annual getaway to commemorate your relationship or as personal as renewing your vows in intimate settings. The key is in the intentional act of setting aside time and space to celebrate your journey together and recommit to the future. These rituals serve as poignant reminders of your shared history and the love that has grown and evolved over time. They can be particularly comforting during times when you feel distant or disconnected, acting as a touchstone to your shared commitment and love.

Navigating Change Together

Change is an inevitable part of life and relationships. Whether it's a career change, the arrival of children, or personal transformations, navigating these changes together is crucial. Strategies for maintaining a united front include maintaining open lines of communication, being flexible with each other's evolving needs, and supporting each other through transitions. For instance, if one partner decides to go back to school, discussing how this change will affect your daily routines, financial situation, and time together is essential. By proactively addressing the implications of this change, you can manage expectations and support each other, reinforcing your partnership even amidst significant life shifts.

Commitment as a Choice

Perhaps the most powerful perspective to adopt during turbulent times is seeing commitment not as a one-time decision but as a choice that is continuously made. Every day, in both small gestures and big decisions, you choose to prioritize your relationship. This perspective empowers you to see beyond the immediate difficulties and appreciate the ongoing investment you both make in your shared life. It underscores the dynamic nature of commitment, where each partner must actively choose to nurture the relationship, adapt to each other's growth, and support one another through life's inevitable ups and downs.

In embracing these strategies, you not only navigate rough patches more effectively but also weave a deeper, more resilient bond that can hold firm against the shifting tides of life. Each challenge becomes a thread in the larger tapestry of your relationship, rich with lessons and victories that contribute to a more profound, enduring love.

In summarizing the essence of renewing commitment in long-term relationships, it's clear that the challenges you face together are not merely obstacles but are, in fact, opportunities to strengthen and deepen your bond. By adopting strategies that transform these trials into avenues for growth, creating meaningful rituals to reaffirm your commitment, navigating life's changes hand-in-hand, and recognizing the active, daily nature of commitment, you ensure that your relationship not only survives but continues to thrive. As we turn the page to the next chapter, we'll explore further into the dynamics of resolving conflicts and ensuring that the communication within your relationship remains open, respectful, and enriching.

Chapter 8

Fostering Healthy Relationship Dynamics

Picture your relationship as a delicate dance, where each step, twirl, and pause is performed not alone but with a partner whose rhythm is uniquely their own. This dance of love, intricate and beautiful, requires an understanding of when to lead and when to follow, creating a harmony that resonates with the music of your joint lives. In this chapter, we delve into the nuanced art of giving and receiving in love—a fundamental aspect that sustains and enriches your relationship, ensuring the dance continues smoothly even when the music changes.

The Art of Giving and Receiving in Love

Balance in Relationships

In any relationship, the exchange of love, support, and care must find a certain equilibrium. Think of it as a seesaw, where both sides need to be equally weighted to maintain a level that feels right and fair. When this balance is off—when one partner consistently gives more than they receive or vice versa—it can foster resentment or feelings of inadequacy, which may slowly erode the relationship's foundation. Achieving this balance does not mean keeping a score but rather fostering an environment where both partners feel equally valued and cared for. It's about recognizing each other's needs and striving to meet them with kindness and generosity, ensuring that no one feels overburdened or neglected. This balance isn't static; it shifts and changes as you both grow and evolve, and part of maintaining a healthy relationship is being attentive and responsive to these changing dynamics.

Understanding Love Languages

The concept of 'love languages' is a helpful tool in enhancing relationship dynamics. Developed by Dr. Gary Chapman, the theory proposes that each person has a primary love language that dictates how they prefer to receive love. The five love languages are Words of Affirmation, Acts of Service, Gift receiving, Quality Time, and Physical Touch. By understanding and speaking your partner's love language, you can express your love toward them in ways that are most meaningful to them. For example, if your partner's primary love language is Acts of Service, they might feel most loved when you help out with daily chores or take on responsibilities that ease their burden. Conversely, if yours is Words of Affirmation, you feel cherished when your partner vocalizes their love and appreciation for you. Learning to 'speak' each other's love languages can transform your relationship, making each gesture of love more impactful and cherished.

Gratitude and Appreciation

Expressing gratitude and appreciation are the threads that weave strength and warmth into the fabric of your relationship. In the busyness of life, the small acts of kindness and support that your partner offers can sometimes go unnoticed or unacknowledged, leading to feelings of being taken for granted. By actively expressing gratitude—whether through words, a note, or a simple hug—you acknowledge and value your partner's actions and presence in your life. This practice not only uplifts their spirit but also reinforces their bond and deepens their connection. It's a simple yet profound way to keep the emotional climate of your relationship positive and affirming.

Practicing Generosity

Generosity in relationships extends beyond the materialistic aspect of giving gifts. It encompasses a broader spectrum that includes being generous with your time, your attention, and your emotional support. This kind of generosity is about willingly sharing parts of your life and yourself with your partner. It's about being generous in forgiving mistakes, offering support during tough times, and sharing joy during moments of celebration. When both partners practice this kind of generous spirit, the relationship becomes a source of incredible strength and comfort for both, providing a safe harbor in the tumultuous seas of life.

Reflection Section

Reflect on your current practices in giving and receiving within your relationship:

- How well do you feel you understand your partner's love language? Are there ways you could more effectively show your love according to their language?
- When was the last time you expressed gratitude for something small your partner did? How can you make this expression of gratitude a more regular part of your relationship?
- Consider your recent acts of generosity. Are there other

ways you might give of yourself to enhance the bond between you and your partner?

Engaging with these questions can help you deepen your understanding and appreciation of your partner, strengthening the dynamic of giving and receiving that is so crucial to a loving, lasting relationship. As you reflect on these aspects, consider the subtle ways in which you can enhance these practices, enriching the dance of your relationship with every thoughtful step and turn.

Detoxing from Codependency: Steps to Independence

In the intricate dance of relationships, maintaining an equal partnership where both individuals support each other without losing their sense of self can be challenging. Codependency often creeps in quietly, masquerading as just being helpful or deeply in love. It's when this helping becomes compulsive, and your emotional state is entirely contingent upon the relationship, that codependency becomes apparent and potentially harmful. Recognizing these patterns is your first step towards cultivating a healthier dynamic where you can love deeply but not at the cost of your own independence.

Codependency often manifests as a reliance on your partner for approval and identity. You might find yourself constantly making sacrifices to please your partner or feeling anxious about their approval. Your own needs and desires might take a back seat as the relationship consumes more of your identity. Recognizing this pattern involves a deep and sometimes uncomfortable introspection. Reflect on your relationship: Are you able to say no without feeling guilty? Do your partner's needs dictate your own actions and emotions? Answering these questions can be a revealing first step in understanding how deeply codependency affects your interactions and sense of self.

Building self-reliance is a crucial next step in this process. It involves reconnecting with your interests, desires, and goals. It's about making decisions that are genuinely in your best interest, not just to appease or please someone else. Start small: engage in activities that you enjoy alone. It could be anything from reading a book to attending a class you've been interested in. The goal is to rebuild your sense of self as an individual, not just as a partner in a relationship. Financial independence is also crucial. If possible, ensure that you have your own resources and are involved in the household's financial decisions. This aspect of independence is essential for reducing vulnerability and building confidence in your ability to support and sustain yourself.

Understanding the difference between unhealthy codependence and healthy interdependence is vital in this journey. While codependency involves an excessive emotional or psychological reliance on a partner, interdependence is a mutual reliance that respects individual autonomy. In a healthy interdependent relationship, both partners maintain their own identities and are able to function independently, but they also support each other and work together. This balance promotes personal growth and relationship satisfaction. Have an open conversation with your partner about your needs for independence and how you can both support each other's growth. This might involve setting some new boundaries or renegotiating old ones.

Recovering from codependency requires patience and, often, a significant amount of emotional work. It might involve setting new boundaries that initially feel uncomfortable or seeking therapy to address deeper issues driving your codependent behaviors. Therapy can be extremely helpful as it provides a supportive space to explore your emotions, understand your relational patterns, and develop healthier ways of interacting. Consider engaging in couple's therapy if both partners are willing—it can help you both understand the dynamics of your relationship better and develop healthier ways of connecting.

Remember, the goal of this recovery is not to make you less caring or supportive but to ensure that your caring does not come at the expense of your own health and happiness.

As you continue to work on these aspects, you will start to find that your relationships become more fulfilling. You will be able to love and support others, but you'll also be able to meet your own needs and pursue your own goals with confidence. Embracing this balanced approach leads to deeper satisfaction and a more profound sense of self-worth, both individually and in your relationships.

Recognizing and Choosing Emotionally Available Partners

In the realm of relationships, the heart's endeavors to connect deeply and meaningfully are often hindered or facilitated by the emotional availability of the individuals involved. Understanding what emotional availability looks like, recognizing its presence or absence in potential partners, and cultivating it within yourself are crucial steps in fostering relationships that are not only satisfying but also nurturing and resilient. Emotional availability in a partner is characterized by a readiness and ability to share emotions openly, to engage in genuine communication about feelings, and to make a concerted effort to understand and connect with your emotional world.

Identifying signs of emotional availability involves observing how a person communicates and responds in various situations. An emotionally available partner often expresses their feelings clearly and respectfully, listens attentively to what you are saying without rushing to solve or dismiss your concerns, and shows a consistent willingness to work through conflicts rather than avoiding them. They are present during interactions, meaning they are not consistently distracted or preoccupied in a way that prevents them from connecting with you. Moreover, such individuals will show genuine interest in your life, your feelings, and your well-being, and their actions will align with their words, demonstrating reliability and commitment.

Attracting emotionally available partners starts with being emotionally available yourself. Reflect on how you express your emotions and handle vulnerability. Are you open and honest about your feelings, or do you find yourself holding back due to fear of being judged or rejected? Working towards greater emotional openness can be challenging, especially if past experiences have made you wary or if your attachment style leans towards the anxious. Engaging in personal development practices such as therapy, mindfulness, and emotional intelligence exercises can enhance your ability to communicate your emotions clearly and confidently. This self-development not only makes you more emotionally attractive but also increases your ability to discern emotional availability in others as you become more familiar with what genuine emotional expression looks and feels like.

Avoiding emotional unavailability requires a keen sense of awareness and the courage to set boundaries. Be wary of individuals who consistently avoid deep conversations, who deflect or minimize discussions about feelings, or whose actions fail to match their words. Emotional unavailability can sometimes be masked by charm or intensity in the early stages of a relationship, making it crucial to look beyond surface-level interactions and pay attention to patterns that emerge over time. If you notice ongoing signs of emotional unavailability, consider addressing these observations directly with the person involved. Clear communication about your needs and observations can either prompt a positive change or clarify the need for you to reconsider the relationship's potential to meet your emotional needs.

Building your emotional availability is an ongoing process that enhances not just romantic relationships but all areas of social interaction. It involves cultivating a deep understanding of your emotions, practicing expressing your feelings in healthy ways, and developing empathy for others' experiences and feelings. Techniques such as journaling can help you articulate your emotions more clearly while engaging in open, vulnerable conversations with trusted friends or family can improve your comfort with emotional expression. Additionally, consider participating in workshops or therapy focused on emotional growth, which can provide valuable tools and insights for enhancing emotional availability.

In essence, choosing an emotionally available partner and becoming one yourself are intertwined processes that require intentionality, self-awareness, and continuous growth. As you enhance your emotional availability, you naturally attract and are drawn to individuals who are similarly open and responsive, paving the way for relationships that are rich in understanding, support, and genuine connection. In this way, the dance of emotional exchange becomes a harmonious and enriching part of your relationship dynamic, allowing love to flourish on a deeply secure and satisfying foundation.

Dealing with Ghosting and Uncertainty in Dating

Understanding Ghosting

In the modern dating landscape, ghosting represents a sudden and unexplained cessation of communication by one party toward another, particularly in the context of an online or budding relationship. This phenomenon leaves the ghosted individual grappling with silence, without closure or an understanding of what went wrong. For someone with an anxious attachment style, ghosting can be particularly harrowing. The lack of closure can trigger deep-seated fears of abandonment and unworthiness, catalyzing a whirlwind of self-doubt and obsessive overthinking about the reasons behind the sudden disconnection. The psychological impact is profound because it not only disrupts external communication but also violently shakes one's internal stability, leaving you to question your value and the authenticity of the connections you form. The abrupt end to what might have seemed like a promising connection can feel like a stark betrayal, intensifying feelings of vulnerability and mistrust toward new relationships.

Coping Mechanisms

When faced with the pain and uncertainty of ghosting, developing effective coping mechanisms is crucial to safeguard your emotional well-being. First and foremost, it's vital to externalize the experience, understanding that someone else's inability to communicate does not reflect your worth or desirability. Reaching out to friends, family, or a support group can provide you with a necessary outlet to express your feelings and gain perspective. Often, simply vocalizing your frustrations and hurt can help dilute the intensity of your emotions. Engaging in self-care practices is also paramount; this can include activities that nourish both your body and soul, such as yoga, meditation, or creative pursuits like art or writing, which can serve as therapeutic outlets for your emotions. Importantly, setting boundaries around your engagement with dating apps or social media post-ghosting can prevent you from spiraling into harmful patterns of stalking or over-analyzing your last interactions. Limiting exposure to the digital presence of the person who ghosted you helps you regain a sense of control and focus on your well-being.

Building Resilience

Building emotional resilience in the face of ghosting and the inherent uncertainties of modern dating is another critical aspect of navigating these challenges. Resilience in this context means developing a robust sense of self that remains stable and strong, regardless of others' actions or validations. Start by affirming your self-worth through positive affirmations that reinforce your qualities and strengths, irrespective of your dating experiences. Regularly engaging in activities that boost your confidence and self-esteem can fortify your emotional defenses against the unpredictability of dating dynamics. Additionally, practicing mindfulness can enhance your resilience by helping you stay grounded in the present moment, decreasing anxiety about future uncertainties, and minimizing rumination about past interactions. Mindfulness practices encourage a compassionate acceptance of your emotional experiences, promoting a balanced perspective that appreciates the present without being overshadowed by past hurts or future fears.

Navigating Uncertainty

Navigating the uncertainties of dating without succumbing to anxiety involves setting realistic expectations about what dating can and cannot offer. Recognize that while dating can be a pathway to meaningful connections, it is also fraught with unpredictability, which does not necessarily reflect your personal failings or worth. Keeping this perspective helps mitigate feelings of disappointment when encounters don't unfold as hoped. Furthermore, actively cultivating interests and relationships outside of dating can provide a fulfilling and balanced life that isn't disproportionately affected by dating successes or setbacks. This diversified investment in various aspects of your life builds a supportive network and enriches your self-identity, reducing the pressure and disappointment associated with dating uncertainties. Lastly, integrating practices such as journaling can be instrumental in processing emotions and maintaining clarity about your dating goals and experiences. By regularly reflecting on your dating interactions and the feelings they evoke, you can maintain a clearer, more centered approach to the highs and lows of dating life.

Incorporating these strategies into your dating life not only helps you cope with the challenges of ghosting and uncertainties but also empowers you to approach dating with confidence, self-respect, and emotional clarity. This proactive stance enhances your interactions and the quality of your dating experiences, fostering a healthier, more optimistic outlook on forming romantic connections.

Breakup Recovery: Moving Forward with Grace and Strength

Grieving the Loss

When a relationship ends, it's as if a curtain falls on a significant part of your life story, leaving behind a stage filled with memories and emotions. It's natural to experience a tumult of feelings: sadness, anger, relief, confusion, and sometimes all at once. Acknowledging this grief is crucial, not as a sign of weakness, but as a necessary process of coming to terms with the loss. Like waves crashing on a shore, emotions can overwhelm you unexpectedly. It's important to allow these feelings to surface without judgment. This might mean crying when you need to, opening up about your feelings with a trusted friend or therapist, or expressing your emotions through art or writing. Remember, there is no "right" way to feel during a breakup. Each relationship is unique, and so is each breakup. What matters is that you permit yourself to feel whatever comes up, recognizing that these emotions are part of healing. During this period, try to avoid making any major decisions or drastic changes to your life. This is a time for reflection and healing, not for immediate action.

Self-Care Post-Breakup

In the aftermath of a breakup, self-care is more than a luxury—it's an act of survival. It's crucial to look after your physical, emotional, and mental health. Start by maintaining basic routines that support your well-being, such as a regular sleep schedule, nutritious meals, and some form of physical activity, even if it's just a walk around the block. These routines can provide a sense of normalcy and control amidst the chaos of emotional upheaval. Additionally, take part in activities that nurture your soul and bring you comfort, whether it's reading, watching your favorite movies, or spending time in nature. Consider practices that promote relaxation and mindfulness, such as yoga, meditation, and deep breathing techniques, to help you manage stress and anxiety. It's also helpful to temporarily distance yourself from mutual friends or social media connections with your ex-partner to protect your emotional space. Instead, lean on supportive friends and family who can provide comfort and perspective during this challenging time. Remember, self-care isn't selfish. It's a necessary foundation for healing and rebuilding your life after a breakup.

Rediscovering yourself

A significant breakup often leaves you questioning not just your relationship but your identity without it. This period of rediscovery is a powerful opportunity to reconnect with yourself and explore the parts of your life that were maybe overshadowed by the relationship. Reflect on your interests, goals, and values—what truly makes you happy and fulfilled? Consider reconnecting with old hobbies that you might have neglected or explore new interests that excite you. This can be an ideal time to set personal goals, whether they're related to career, education, health, or personal projects. Partake in activities that build your confidence and self-esteem, such as taking on new challenges at work or joining a class that interests you. This process of rediscovery can be exhilarating—it's a journey back to your own needs, desires, and aspirations, which can lead to a profound sense of renewal and self-confidence. Remember, you are complete on your own, and this period is about embracing and celebrating the person you are, independently of anyone else.

Moving Forward

Moving forward after a breakup means gradually opening your heart and life to new possibilities. It doesn't require rushing into new romantic relationships; rather, it's about embracing life's myriad opportunities for growth and happiness. Begin by setting small, achievable goals that motivate you and give you something to look forward to. It could be as simple as planning a trip with friends, starting a new project, or volunteering for a cause you care about. These activities not only enrich your life but also help shift your focus from the past to the future. As you begin to feel more grounded, consider expanding your social circle. Meeting new people—whether for friendship or dating—can be refreshing and affirming. Take it slow, allowing yourself to open up to new relationships gradually. Trust that with time, your heart will heal, and you'll be ready to welcome new experiences and connections with openness and optimism. Remember, every ending is also a beginning, and each step forward is a step toward a new chapter of your life, filled with potential for joy and discovery.

When to Hold On and When to Let Go

Understanding when to deepen your commitment and when to release and move on can often feel like navigating a complex maze without a clear map in the landscape of relationships. This part of your relationship journey requires introspection and a clear-eyed assessment of the health and direction of your partnership. Evaluating the health of your relationship is not merely about tallying good moments against bad but involves a deeper analysis of whether your relationship fundamentally enriches your life and aligns with your growth and well-being.

To start, consider the mutual respect, support, and joy you share. These are cornerstones of a healthy relationship. Ask yourself: Do we treat each other with consideration and kindness, even during disagreements? Is there a mutual effort to support each other's dreams and cope with life's challenges together? Relationships that score high on these aspects are often worth investing in despite the inevitable ups and downs. However, it's also crucial to be honest about recurring patterns that may be detrimental. Signs that it might be time to let go include persistent disrespect, unresolved conflicts that recycle the same grievances, and a general decline in emotional connection that efforts at rejuvenation do not seem to mend. If your relationship consistently leaves you feeling drained, undervalued, or stifled in your personal growth, these are significant indicators that the relationship may not be conducive to your well-being.

Holding on with purpose is about actively choosing to work on your relationship through conscious efforts and strategies aimed at resolving issues and enhancing your bond. This choice is grounded in the belief that the relationship is fundamentally sound but currently faces challenges that are surmountable with joint effort. It involves open communication where both partners can communicate their needs and fears without fear of judgment or retaliation. It might also include seeking help from a couples' therapist to provide guidance and tools to navigate through your issues more effectively. The decision to hold on is a commitment to the process of growth and healing together, recognizing that all relationships go through seasons and that challenges can be a gateway to deeper understanding and intimacy.

Navigating breakups with compassion and grace is crucial, especially when it becomes clear that parting ways is the healthiest choice. Ending a relationship, particularly a long-term one, can feel like uprooting a part of your life. It's important to approach this process with kindness and respect for both your partner and yourself. Communicate your feelings and decisions clearly and respectfully, avoiding blame and focusing instead on your feelings and needs. Allow yourself and your partner the space to process the breakup emotionally. Surround yourself with a support system of friends and family who can provide comfort and perspective during this transition. Moreover, engage in self-care practices that reinforce your well-being and help you navigate through the emotional complexities of a breakup.

In concluding this exploration of when to hold on and when to let go, remember that the decision is deeply personal and influenced by unique factors specific to your relationship. Whether choosing to invest more deeply in your relationship or to part ways, the guiding principles should always be respect, honesty, and a clear alignment with your personal growth and happiness. Moving forward, the insights gained from this process can empower you to foster healthier and more fulfilling relationships in the future, whether with a current or a new partner.

Transitioning from understanding when to hold on and let go, the next chapter will explore the ongoing journey of fostering personal growth and happiness within and outside of relationships. This next section will provide you with strategies and insights on enriching your personal life, ensuring that your happiness and growth continue, irrespective of your relationship status.

Chapter 9

Tools for Everyday Anxieties

In the intricate ballet of daily life, high-stress situations are like unexpected, brisk tempo changes that can disrupt your rhythm, leaving you feeling off-balance and anxious. Whether it's a looming deadline, a public speaking engagement, or a personal conflict, these moments test your ability to maintain composure and clarity. Understanding how to navigate these high-stress waters with grace and effectiveness is not just about alleviating immediate discomfort; it's about cultivating a resilience that enriches your overall quality of life, ensuring you are prepared to meet challenges with confidence rather than apprehension.

Managing Anxiety in High-Stress Situations

Identifying Stress Triggers

Recognizing what triggers your anxiety in high-stress situations is akin to a dancer understanding their body's limitations and strengths. It is a critical first step in managing your responses and requires an honest self-assessment. Triggers can vary widely; they may include specific people, environments, or tasks that overwhelm your sense of control or evoke past traumas. To identify these triggers, start by monitoring your physical and emotional responses in different scenarios. Do you notice a rapid heartbeat, sweating, or a sense of dread when asked to speak in front of a group? Do tight deadlines cause you to panic or procrastinate? Keeping a log of such observations can help you connect the dots between your reactions and the triggering situations. This awareness is empowering—it shifts you from a reactive posture to one where you can anticipate and strategize your responses.

Stress-Reduction Techniques

Once triggers are identified, employing stress-reduction techniques can significantly alleviate your anxiety. It can be quite helpful to use methods like gradual muscle relaxation, guided visualization, and deep breathing. For instance, before a stressful event, you might spend a few minutes in a quiet space practicing deep breathing exercises. This involves inhaling deeply through your nose, holding your breath for a few seconds, and then slowly exhaling through your mouth. This simple practice can help reduce cortisol levels, lower your heart rate, and clear your mind, equipping you to handle the impending challenge with greater calmness and clarity. Additionally, techniques like progressive muscle relaxation, where you tense and relax different muscle groups, can be particularly effective in releasing the physical tension that accompanies anxiety.

Preparation and Practice

"Practice makes perfect" is a time-honored truth, particularly when it comes to managing anxiety in high-stress situations. Preparation can take various forms, from rehearsing a presentation multiple times to mapping out deadlines for a project to avoid last-minute rushes. The key is to simulate the stress-inducing experience as closely as possible during your preparation phase. For example, if public speaking triggers anxiety, try rehearsing your speech in front of friends or even in front of a mirror, gradually increasing the number of people as you become more confident. This not only familiarizes you with the content but also with the experience of being observed while speaking, reducing the novelty and associated stress on the actual day.

Seeking Support

Finally, do not underestimate the power of seeking support when facing high-stress situations. Sharing your apprehensions with a trusted friend, family member, or mentor can provide not only emotional comfort but also practical advice on how to handle the situation. Sometimes, just vocalizing your fears can diminish their power and make them more manageable. If the anxiety feels overwhelming, consider seeking support from a professional therapist who can provide tailored strategies to cope with stress effectively. Engaging with support groups where members share similar experiences can also offer reassurance and practical tips for managing stress.

Incorporating these strategies into your approach to high-stress situations transforms your experience from one of dread and anxiety to one of competence and calmness. With each application, your confidence grows, and what once seemed daunting becomes a well-rehearsed routine that you are well-equipped to handle. As these practices become integrated into your daily life, you'll find that your ability to dance through life's stresses, not merely stumble through them, significantly enhances your overall well-being and satisfaction.

Journaling for Self-Discovery and Healing

Journaling, a simple yet profound tool, can be your sanctuary for self-discovery and emotional healing. By transferring thoughts from mind to paper, you create a space to explore your inner world, making sense of feelings and events that often go unexamined. This process is particularly valuable if you find yourself caught in the whirlpool of anxious attachment, where fears and uncertainties about relationships can feel overwhelming. Let's explore how different types of journaling can cater to various aspects of your personal journey toward understanding and healing your attachment style.

Reflective journaling, for instance, is a powerful method to delve into the deeper layers of your emotions and reactions. This type of journaling involves looking back at your day or a specific event and writing about it with an emphasis on how you felt and reacted. Imagine you had a day where you felt particularly needy or insecure in your relationship; reflective journaling allows you to explore these feelings in a safe, private space. You might ask yourself what triggered these feelings, how you responded, and how you might handle a similar situation differently in the future. This practice not only aids in self-awareness but also in regulating emotions and changing reactive patterns over time.

Gratitude journaling, on the other hand, shifts your focus from anxieties and fears to appreciation and positivity. By regularly writing down things you are grateful for, you can teach your mind to recognize and appreciate the good in your life, which can often be overshadowed by anxieties about relationships. Even on tough days, finding small elements of joy—maybe a friend's supportive message, a delicious meal, or simply a moment of quiet—can uplift your spirits and gradually alter your overall perspective toward life and relationships.

Future scripting is another transformative journaling practice, especially for those dealing with anxious attachment. It involves writing about your future as if you've already achieved your goals of secure attachment and fulfilling relationships. Describe your ideal day, how you interact with your partner, and how you manage disagreements or stress. This method not only clarifies what you aspire to achieve in your relationships but also boosts your motivation and confidence to work towards these goals, providing a mental blueprint that guides your actions and decisions.

Journaling Prompts for Anxious Attachment

To specifically address anxious attachment, journaling prompts can be tailored to untangle the complex feelings associated with this style. Consider prompts like, "What does security in a relationship mean to me?" or "When do I feel most anxious in a relationship and why?" These questions encourage you to think critically and deeply about your fears, desires, and patterns, facilitating a better understanding of your attachment style and how it affects your relationships. Other prompts might include, "How do I typically express my needs to my partner, and how are they received?" or "What are my core beliefs about love and trust, and where do they come from?" By regularly engaging with these prompts, you develop a clearer picture of your relational dynamics and how your attachment style plays out in everyday interactions.

The Process of Reflection

Regularly engaging in journaling can dramatically enhance your understanding of your attachment patterns and behaviors. The act of writing slows down your thought processes and provides a moment of pause to reflect on your actions and reactions. This reflective process is crucial in identifying and modifying patterns that may be detrimental to your relationships. As you write, you begin to see connections between your thoughts, feelings, and behaviors, some of which may have been previously obscured by the immediacy of emotional reactions. Over time, this ongoing reflective practice can lead to profound insights and significant changes in how you relate to others, fostering healthier, more secure attachment behaviors.

Privacy and Honesty

For journaling to be effective, especially in the delicate area of personal attachments and relationships, honesty is non-negotiable. To ensure that you can be completely honest in your journal, it's essential to keep it private. This is your personal space, free from the eyes and judgments of others. Consider using a journal with a lock or keeping it in a private place to safeguard your thoughts. The assurance of privacy empowers you to express your deepest fears, wildest dreams, and genuine thoughts without censorship. This uninhibited self-expression is key to uncovering the true nature of your thoughts and feelings, which is the cornerstone of genuine self-discovery and healing.

By incorporating these journaling practices into your routine, you can gain a powerful tool for understanding and transforming your patterns of anxious attachment. Each page you fill not only documents your journey but also paves the way for greater self-awareness, emotional healing, and, ultimately, the development of healthier, more secure ways of connecting with those you love.

The Role of Physical Activity in Anxiety Reduction

Imagine yourself embracing the rhythmic movements of your body, each step or stretch melting away layers of anxiety, leaving you lighter and more at peace. This isn't just a pleasant visualization; it's rooted in the well-documented benefits of physical activity on mental health. When you engage in exercise, your body releases chemicals known as endorphins. Often referred to as the body's organic painkillers, endorphins also play a crucial role in elevating mood and alleviating stress. This chemical uplift isn't merely temporary relief but can contribute to an impactful and lasting reduction in anxiety levels. For someone grappling with the constant worries and fears characteristic of anxious attachment, regular physical activity can become a vital part of your toolkit, not only for managing anxiety but also for enhancing overall well-being.

Choosing the right type of physical activity is crucial because the best exercise for reducing anxiety is the one you will consistently perform and enjoy. The options are as varied as they are enjoyable. You might find solace in the steady, rhythmic cadence of a long walk, the focused strength required for climbing, or the exhilarating freedom of swimming. Each activity offers unique benefits, but they all share the common feature of redirecting your focus from anxious thoughts to the physical task at hand. Experimenting with different activities can be an exciting journey of discovery, one where you not only learn what your body prefers but also what quiets your mind most effectively. For instance, if solitude and contemplation help you unwind, solo activities like running or cycling might be most beneficial. Conversely, if social interaction lightens your spirits, consider joining a dance class or a local sports team. The key is to listen to your body and your emotional responses to different activities, allowing your preferences and enjoyment to guide your choices.

While engaging in any form of exercise is beneficial, the consistency of your physical activity is more impactful than the intensity. Integrating moderate exercise into your routine several times a week is more effective in managing anxiety than occasional, intense workouts that can actually raise stress levels if they feel like a chore or a strain. Implementing a routine that fits seamlessly into your daily life is crucial. This could be as simple as a morning yoga session, a lunchtime walk, or an evening bike ride. The regularity of these activities provides a rhythmic anchor for your day, something to look forward to that you know will bring relief and joy. Over time, this consistency not only cultivates physical fitness but also builds emotional resilience, turning the tide against anxiety with each session.

Incorporating mindfulness into your exercise routine can boost the connection between mind and body, offering a double dose of anxiety relief. Mindful movement-based activities like yoga and tai chi are especially effective in this regard, as they combine physical activity with an intentional focus on breath and movement. These practices encourage you to stay present in the moment, an antidote to the often future-focused worries of anxious attachment. As you move through different poses or sequences, your attention is drawn to the alignment of your body, the rhythm of your breathing, and the sensations of each movement. This mindful movement is a form of meditation in motion, providing a tranquil space for your mind to rest while your body is active. The dual focus on breath and movement enhances your ability to control physiological responses to stress, making you better equipped to handle anxiety in everyday situations.

Through regular, enjoyable physical activity tailored to your preferences, combined with the mindful connection of movement and breath, you can transform your relationship with anxiety. Each step, each stretch, and each breath is not just a move towards physical health but a stride towards a calmer, more centered you. As you continue to integrate these practices into your life, they become more than just exercises; they evolve into rituals of self-care that fortify your mental resilience and enrich your journey toward emotional stability.

Nutrition and Mental Health: What You Need to Know

Understanding the intricate link between what you eat and how you feel can be a game-changer, especially when grappling with the anxieties that come with a preoccupied attachment style. The gut-brain axis serves as a bi-directional communication line between your gastrointestinal tract and your brain, with each influencing the other. It's fascinating to consider that your digestive system doesn't just help with food but also plays an important role in regulating emotions and mental health. This connection is primarily mediated by the vagus nerve, one of the longest nerves found in your body, which sends signals in both directions. For instance, stress can slow down digestion, leading to gastrointestinal issues, while conversely, an imbalance in your gut flora can lead to an increase in stress and anxiety levels.

Foods that positively impact your gut health can, in turn, enhance your mood and decrease anxiety. Adding food items with omega-3 fatty acids, like salmon, flaxseeds, and walnuts, to your diet is particularly beneficial. Omega-3s are key for brain health and are linked with lowered rates of depression and anxiety. These fatty acids help build brain and nerve cells, which are essential for cognitive functions and emotional health. Antioxidants found in fruits such as blueberries, strawberries, and oranges or vegetables like kale and bell peppers help combat oxidative stress—an imbalance of free radicals and antioxidants in your body, which can be exacerbated by stress. Probiotics, found in yogurt, sauerkraut, and other fermented foods, help contribute to a healthy gut microbiome, which studies have shown to be crucial in influencing mood regulation.

Hydration plays an often-understated role in managing anxiety and maintaining emotional balance. Dehydration can lead to increased cortisol levels, the stress hormone, which may make managing anxiety more challenging. Ensuring you're adequately hydrated helps maintain cortisol levels and supports overall brain function, including mood regulation and stress management. Simple habits like starting your day with a glass of water, carrying a water bottle throughout the day, and opting for hydrating foods like cucumbers, celery, and watermelon can significantly boost your hydration levels.

Creating a balanced diet is more than just choosing the right foods; it's about making meal plans that support your mental health and fit seamlessly into your life. This involves incorporating a variety of nutrients that support brain health, managing portion sizes to avoid overeating, and being mindful of your eating habits to ensure they contribute to a balanced mood. Begin by including a source of lean protein in every meal, which can help regulate your blood sugar levels and, thus, your mood. Carbohydrates like whole grains, legumes, and vegetables can boost serotonin levels, a neurotransmitter that enhances your mood and has a calming effect. Planning your meals can also help manage cravings by ensuring you have healthy options available when you're hungry, reducing the likelihood of reaching for sugary snacks that can lead to mood swings.

By understanding and applying the principles of nutrition and mental health, you can effectively enhance your mood, decrease anxiety, and support your overall well-being through mindful eating. This approach doesn't just ease the symptoms associated with anxious attachment but enriches your overall quality of life, providing a strong and nourished foundation from which to interact with the world and your relationships.

Rewiring Your Brain: Techniques for Positive Thinking

In the landscape of your mind, the paths you frequently travel can become deeply etched, guiding your thoughts and reactions often without conscious effort. This is the essence of neuroplasticity—the brain's remarkable ability to reorganize itself by developing new neural connections throughout life. This adaptability means that with consistent practice, you can cultivate new, healthier patterns of thought that support a more secure attachment style and a more joyful, resilient approach to relationships and life.

Positive affirmations are a potent tool in this transformative process. These are positive, first-person statements that you repeat to yourself, designed to challenge and undermine negative beliefs and to reinforce positive self-perception and confidence. For instance, changing a thought from "I am always going to be alone" to "I am deserving of love and capable of forming healthy relationships" can gradually rewire your thought patterns. It's like planting flowers in a well-trodden path of weeds—the more you nurture these positive thoughts, the more robust they become. To integrate affirmations into your daily routine, start by identifying negative self-talk or beliefs that frequently arise, especially those linked to your anxious attachment tendencies. Craft affirmations that directly counter these negative thoughts and schedule regular times to recite them, perhaps in the morning before you start your day or in the evening as you reflect. Over time, these affirmations can shift your mindset from one of self-doubt and fear to one of confidence and hope.

Cognitive behavioral therapy (CBT) is another cornerstone in the architecture of mind reshaping. CBT is rooted in the concept that your thoughts, feelings, and behaviors are interconnected. It states that changing negative thought patterns can improve your emotions and actions. This approach involves identifying specific negative thought patterns that contribute to your anxiety, challenging their validity, and replacing them with more balanced, healthy thoughts. For example, if you often find yourself catastrophizing in your relationship—expecting the worst outcome from minor disagreements—you can use CBT techniques to question the evidence supporting these catastrophic predictions, assess their likelihood, and develop more balanced perspectives. Engaging in such cognitive exercises regularly teaches you to approach relationship challenges with a clearer, more balanced mindset, reducing anxiety and fostering healthier interactions.

Visualizing secure attachment involves creating detailed mental images of yourself in a securely attached relationship. Visualization leverages the brain's neuroplasticity by repeatedly simulating positive relationship experiences, which can help reinforce secure attachment behaviors. Picture scenarios where you feel safe, valued and connected to your partner. Imagine handling conflicts calmly, expressing your needs clearly, and receiving support and understanding. Feel the emotions associated with these positive interactions deeply—contentment, safety, and connection. By regularly practicing this visualization, you can begin to shift your expectations and behaviors in relationships from anxious to secure, essentially training your brain to adopt these healthier patterns in real-life interactions.

Incorporating these techniques into your daily life isn't just about reducing anxiety or transforming your attachment style; it's about fundamentally enhancing your quality of life. By rewiring your brain to think more positively, react more adaptively, and visualize more constructively, you equip yourself with the tools to not only foster healthier relationships but also to lead a more joyful, fulfilled life.

As you continue to practice these techniques, remember that change takes time and persistence. Each effort you make is a step towards not only transforming your mind but also enriching your relationships and your experiences in the world. With each positive affirmation, each challenge to a negative thought, and each visualization of security and love, you are paving a new, healthier path in your mental landscape. Keep moving forward with patience and confidence, knowing that the journey you are on is reshaping not just your mind but your life.

In exploring the tools for managing everyday anxieties, we've journeyed through practical strategies and profound insights aimed at boosting your mental and emotional well-being. From identifying stress triggers and embracing journaling for deeper self-understanding to engaging in physical activities that joyfully tether mind to body and nourishing yourself with foods that fortify against anxiety, each strategy has been a step toward not just managing anxiety but transforming your engagement with the world. As we close this chapter, remember that each tool and technique offers a unique way to support your journey toward a more peaceful, empowered, and connected life. These practices are not just responses to challenges but proactive steps toward crafting a life filled with more joy, resilience, and fulfillment.

As we transition into the next chapter, we will build upon these foundations, exploring deeper into the realms of personal growth and relationships. Each step forward will carry forward the lessons learned here, ensuring that you are equipped not just to face life's challenges but to thrive amidst them.

Chapter 10

Shadow Work and Anxious Attachment

Introduction to Shadow Work: Healing Hidden Wounds

Imagine you're walking through a dense forest where the light barely touches the ground. Here, in the shadowy underbrush, parts of yourself that you rarely acknowledge—your fears, past traumas, and repressed emotions—lurk quietly. This metaphorical landscape represents the concept of the psychological shadow, a term coined by the famed psychiatrist Carl Jung. It refers to those aspects of our personality that we deny or ignore—parts that are often uncomfortable and challenging but are integral to our personal growth and emotional well-being.

In the context of anxious attachment, these shadows can manifest as fears of abandonment, low self-esteem, or unhealthy relationship patterns that we might not readily acknowledge or understand. Engaging in shadow work, then, involves shining a light into these forested areas of our psyche, confronting these hidden parts of ourselves, and integrating them to achieve a more whole and balanced self. This process is not just about uncovering negative traits or memories but also about discovering untapped strengths and qualities that have been buried under years of emotional neglect or trauma.

The benefits of shadow work are profoundly transformative, particularly for those grappling with anxious attachment. By facing and understanding these darker aspects of your psyche, you can begin to see how they influence your behavior in relationships. For example, recognizing a shadow aspect that clings to partners out of fear of loneliness can lead to a conscious adjustment in how you interact in relationships, fostering healthier dynamics and reducing anxiety. This introspective work can be challenging, often evoking discomfort and resistance, but the growth it fosters can significantly enhance your emotional resilience and lead to more secure and fulfilling relationships.

However, safety is paramount in this explorative process. Shadow-work can dredge up intense emotions and painful memories, making it necessary to approach this work with care. If at any point the process becomes overwhelming, seeking professional support from a therapist skilled in depth psychology can provide the necessary guidance and safeguard your mental health. This professional support is crucial not just for navigating painful memories but also for helping integrate these insights constructively.

As we prepare to embark on this deep, introspective work, it's essential to set realistic expectations. The journey through your psychological shadow is not a quick fix but a gradual process of self-discovery and healing. It requires patience, persistence, and, most importantly, a compassionate attitude towards yourself. Engaging with your shadow is not about self-criticism or dwelling on your faults but about acknowledging all parts of yourself with empathy and understanding. This comprehensive acceptance paves the way for genuine self-love and lasting change.

Reflective Journaling Exercise

To begin engaging with your shadow, consider this journaling exercise: Reflect on a recent situation in a relationship where you felt strong emotions such as jealousy, anger, or fear. Write about the experience in detail, exploring what triggered these emotions and how you reacted. Then, ask yourself what these feelings might be saying about your needs and desires in relationships. This exercise is not just about understanding your emotional reactions but about recognizing the deeper parts of your psyche that influence these reactions. Regularly journaling about such experiences can provide insights into your shadow self, guiding your journey towards healing and wholeness.

Identifying Your Shadow: Exercises for Self-Discovery

Exploring the shadow self can feel much like peering into uncharted territories of your mind, revealing insights that are at once enlightening and challenging. For those of you grappling with anxious attachment, this exploration is particularly potent, offering a pathway to understand the deeper, often hidden drivers behind your relationship dynamics. The exercises designed for this purpose are not only tools for illumination but also for transformation, enabling you to engage with your shadow self in ways that foster profound personal growth.

One fundamental technique in this introspective endeavor is targeted journaling. Unlike standard diary entries, these journal prompts are crafted to coax out the elements of your shadow that directly impact your attachment style. For instance, you might engage with prompts such as, "What am I most afraid of in my relationships?" or "When do I find myself feeling the most insecure, and what thoughts accompany these feelings?" These inquiries encourage you to dig deep into your emotional and mental landscapes, uncovering fears and beliefs about worthiness, abandonment, and intimacy. As you write, you're invited to bypass the superficial layers of your experiences and delve into the core of your emotional framework. This process is not just about reflection—it's about confrontation and acknowledgment, critical steps towards healing and growth.

Another powerful aspect of shadow work involves recognizing and understanding projection. Projection is a defense mechanism where you might attribute personal traits, emotions, or intentions—often unacceptable or undesirable—to others instead of acknowledging them as your own. In relationships, this might look like accusing your partner of not caring enough when, in reality, you are struggling with feelings of unworthiness or fear of being unlovable. Teaching yourself to identify when you are projecting can be transformative. By tracing these projections back to their origins, you can start to see how your shadow influences your perceptions and interactions. This awareness creates a space to respond to relationship challenges with greater clarity and less bias, setting the stage for healthier communication and deeper connections.

Embracing vulnerability is another crucial step in engaging with your shadow. Vulnerability here refers to the willingness to face uncomfortable truths about yourself, to acknowledge and experience difficult emotions without resorting to defense mechanisms. This openness is not indicative of weakness; instead, it's a profound strength that fosters authenticity and deepens connections with others. In the context of shadow work, embracing vulnerability might mean admitting to feelings of jealousy, recognizing patterns of manipulation, or confronting past traumas that shape current behaviors. While this can be daunting, the act of making yourself vulnerable breaks down the barriers erected by your shadow, allowing for true healing and integration to occur.

As you undertake these exercises, remember that the goal is not to eradicate your shadow but to understand and integrate it. This integration is essential for moving towards a more secure attachment style, where relationships are not just about seeking validation or avoiding abandonment but about genuine connection and mutual growth. Through these practices, you're not just exploring the depths of your psyche; you're also laying the groundwork for more fulfilling and resilient relationships that stand the test of time and change.

Shadow Work Techniques for Releasing Old Patterns

In the garden of your mind, old patterns and entrenched beliefs are like weeds that can choke the growth of new, healthier ways of being. These patterns often stem from the shadow side of our psyche, harboring fears and traumas that unconsciously shape our actions and reactions, especially in the realm of relationships. To cultivate a garden—your mind—that nurtures secure attachment and healthy interactions, it becomes essential to clear these weeds systematically. This process involves a series of techniques that not only help in recognizing these patterns but also effectively release them, allowing for new seeds of thought and behavior to take root.

One effective technique for releasing the grip of shadow aspects is through targeted visualizations. This method harnesses the power of your imagination to envision a scenario where you confront a shadow aspect, such as fear of abandonment. Picture yourself in a safe space, perhaps a room that feels comforting and secure. Visualize a figure that represents this fear—notice its shape, its color, and its size. Engage with this figure in a dialogue, asking why it clings so tightly to your psyche. Listen to its concerns and reassure it that you are now capable of finding security within yourself and your relationships. Gradually, imagine the figure shrinking, its color fading, symbolizing its diminishing influence over you. This visualization not only helps in confronting and understanding your fears but also empowers you to mentally and emotionally release them, reducing their unconscious control over your actions.

Affirmations serve as powerful tools in rewriting the internal narratives that often perpetuate anxious attachment. These short, affirmative statements are designed to counteract the negative self-talk that shadows can instigate. Begin by identifying a negative belief that frequently surfaces in your thoughts, perhaps something like, "I am not worthy of lasting love." Transform this into an affirmation that promotes a new belief, such as, "I am inherently worthy of love and capable of fostering healthy, lasting relationships." Repeat this affirmation daily, ideally in front of a mirror, making eye contact with yourself to reinforce the message. Over time, this practice can significantly alter your subconscious beliefs, gradually replacing doubt and fear with confidence and security.

Bodywork, specifically somatic exercises, also plays a crucial role in releasing stored emotions and traumas that contribute to the anxious attachment. Our bodies often hold onto emotional pain in ways that we might not be consciously aware of, manifesting as tension, fatigue, or other physical symptoms. Engaging in somatic exercises can help you connect with these physical manifestations and release them. Techniques such as grounding, where you focus on the physical feeling of your feet touching the ground, or progressive muscle relaxation, where you tense and relax different muscle groups, can be particularly effective. These practices not only bring awareness to bodily sensations associated with emotional pain but also promote a physical release of that pain, helping to alleviate the psychological impact of past traumas.

Forgiveness, both of oneself and others is a pivotal step in the process of healing and releasing old patterns. It involves acknowledging past hurts and traumas, understanding the roles various figures, including oneself, have played in these experiences, and consciously deciding to let go of the associated anger and resentment. Forgiveness does not mean condoning hurtful behaviors or forgetting the pain caused; rather, it is an act of liberating oneself from the burden of past grievances, allowing emotional wounds to heal, and making space for new, healthier experiences. Engage in a forgiveness meditation where you visualize the people you need to forgive, including yourself, and mentally express your forgiveness, wishing them peace and healing. This practice can be profoundly liberating, facilitating a release of the emotional chains that bind you to your past and opening your heart and mind to the potential for new ways of loving and relating.

Through these techniques—visualization, affirmations, bodywork, and forgiveness—you empower yourself to weed out old, limiting patterns and foster a fertile ground for the growth of new, healthy ways of being. Each practice offers a unique approach to engaging with and healing your shadow, gradually leading you toward a more secure and fulfilling way of connecting with yourself and others. As you continue to apply these techniques, remember that each step forward is a step closer to reclaiming your emotional freedom and nurturing more loving, balanced relationships.

Integrating the Shadow: Towards Wholeness and Healing

Integration of the shadow is a profound process where you begin to accept and incorporate the parts of yourself that you've previously ignored or suppressed. It's about acknowledging that these shadow aspects, often sources of pain or discomfort, are also vital components of your entire being. In the context of anxious attachment, integrating your shadow can mean accepting that your fears of abandonment or feelings of unworthiness are part of you, but they do not define you. Through integration, these elements are transformed from disruptive forces into sources of strength and self-awareness, allowing for a more balanced and secure attachment style.

This integration process involves several nuanced steps, each requiring attention and care. Initially, it's about recognizing and acknowledging these shadow aspects. This might mean admitting to yourself that part of your clinginess in relationships stems from deep-seated fears of being alone that you haven't fully accepted. Acknowledgment is followed by understanding—delving into how these traits developed. Perhaps your fear of abandonment originated from early childhood experiences where emotional support was inconsistent. With understanding, you can begin to feel compassion for these parts of yourself, recognizing them as protective mechanisms that your psyche created.

The next step is to start consciously working with these traits. For instance, when you feel the urge to check your partner's messages—a behavior stemming from your shadow's fear of abandonment—pause and consider this impulse. Ask yourself what you're really seeking through this action. Is it reassurance? Security? How might these needs be met in a healthier, more trusting way? This might involve communicating your feelings with your partner or engaging in self-soothing practices that affirm your worth and reduce dependency on external validation.

An essential part of integrating your shadow is creating new narratives about your worth and capabilities in relationships. This might involve shifting from a self-image of someone who is always at risk of being left behind to seeing yourself as a person worthy of love and capable of maintaining healthy, secure bonds. Affirmations can be incredibly helpful here, as can visualization exercises where you imagine yourself handling relationship situations in a secure, confident manner. Over time, these practices help cement the new, integrated self-image—where shadow traits are recognized but don't dominate your actions or self-perception.

Integration is not a one-time thing; it is a continuous process of growth and self-discovery. It requires ongoing attention and adjustment as different situations in life might bring out different aspects of your shadow. Celebrating each step of this integration process is crucial—it's about recognizing and honoring the work you've done to understand and transform your shadow aspects. Each small victory, be it recognizing a trigger or changing a habitual reaction, is a step toward a more secure and authentic self.

Maintaining a balance between light and shadow aspects involves regular self-reflection and mindfulness. It's about continuously engaging with both the strengths and vulnerabilities you possess. Keeping a journal to write your raw thoughts can be an invaluable tool to help you chart your reactions, emotions, and instances where shadow aspects either helped or hindered your interactions. Mindfulness practices can also help you to stay centered and aware, providing the mental clarity needed to see when shadow traits are at play and choose how best to respond.

In relationships, this balance is particularly crucial. It's important to communicate openly with your partner about your shadow work, sharing your discoveries and how they might affect your relationship dynamics. This openness can foster deeper intimacy and understanding, as it invites your partner to share their own personal growth and challenges. Together, you can support each other's journeys, providing empathy and encouragement as you each work to integrate your shadows, leading to a richer, more connected relationship.

By embracing this ongoing process of shadow integration, you actively contribute to your own healing and the health of your relationships. It's a testament to your courage and commitment to becoming the best version of yourself—not by denying your complexities but by embracing and integrating them into a cohesive, empowered whole.

Shadow Work and Relationships: Healing Together

When partners engage in shadow work together, they embark on a profound exploration of not only their individual depths but also the complexities that define their shared life. This mutual journey into shadow work can significantly deepen the connection between partners, as it encourages transparency, vulnerability, and a shared commitment to growth. Understanding and supporting each other's shadow aspects can transform potential conflicts into opportunities for strengthening the relationship.

For couples, shadow work involves a delicate balance of introspection and interaction. It requires each partner to engage with their own shadows while also being receptive and supportive of the other's experiences. This dual engagement can be facilitated through shared exercises designed to uncover and discuss personal fears, desires, and past traumas that influence current relationship dynamics. For instance, partners can take turns sharing aspects of their shadows that they feel most influence their reactions and behaviors within the relationship. This practice not only fosters a deeper understanding of each other's inner landscapes but also cultivates a sense of empathy and support as each partner witnesses and validates the other's vulnerabilities.

Navigating the interplay of individual shadows within the relationship dynamic requires a high degree of emotional intelligence and communication skills. It's crucial for partners to recognize when a conflict or tension might be driven by shadow aspects rather than the immediate circumstances of their interaction. For example, if one partner's shadow includes a deep-seated fear of inadequacy, they might perceive criticism where none was intended. Recognizing such patterns can help couples step back from potential conflicts and approach the situation with a clearer understanding of the underlying emotional triggers. By addressing these deeper issues together, partners can work towards resolutions that acknowledge and integrate these shadow aspects rather than exacerbating them.

The process of shadow integration within a relationship often leads to greater intimacy and understanding. As partners reveal more of their hidden selves and accept each other's flaws and strengths, they build a more authentic connection. This emotional intimacy is deepened when both partners actively engage in healing not just their own shadows but also the relational dynamics that these shadows have influenced. For instance, if both partners have shadows that involve fear of abandonment, they can work together to create a relationship environment that consistently affirms their commitment and care for each other, thereby alleviating mutual fears.

However, engaging in shadow work as a couple also necessitates the setting of healthy boundaries. These boundaries are essential for ensuring that the emotional exploration does not overwhelm either the partner or the relationship itself. Boundaries might include agreeing on specific times to engage in shadow work discussions, using safe words to pause emotionally intense conversations, or even recognizing when it's appropriate to involve a professional therapist. These boundaries ensure that both partners feel safe and respected throughout the process, allowing them to explore their shadows without fear of judgment or emotional injury.

Incorporating shadow work into a relationship is a delicate art that requires patience, understanding, and a strong foundation of trust. As partners learn to navigate their shadows together, they not only enhance their personal growth but also contribute to a more robust, resilient, and intimate relationship. This shared journey through the darker parts of each other's psyches can ultimately light the way to a brighter, more loving future together.

By engaging in this deep, introspective work, partners can reveal and address the underlying issues that often manifest as conflicts, thereby fostering a deeper understanding and stronger bond. As we move forward, the insights and strategies discussed here can serve as a guide for couples who are committed to growing together and strengthening their connection through mutual emotional and psychological exploration. As we conclude this chapter, we transition into further discussions on how these foundational practices influence longer-term dynamics and the ongoing journey of relationship growth.

Chapter 11

Embracing a Secure Future

The Journey from Anxious to Secure Attachment

Understanding the Journey

The transition from anxious to secure attachment doesn't follow a straight line—it meanders, with rises and dips, and each step forward is a piece of the puzzle in understanding yourself and reshaping your relationships. Initially, this path requires a deep dive into self-awareness. It's about recognizing the triggers that spark your anxiety in relationships and understanding the roots of these reactions, which often stretch back to early experiences of uncertainty or inconsistency in love and care.

As you become more aware of these patterns, the next phase involves actively practicing emotional regulation techniques. This could be anything from mindfulness exercises that help you remain present during moments of relationship stress to cognitive-behavioral strategies that aid in restructuring negative thoughts about self-worth and abandonment. The key here is patience and persistence; change is gradual and requires consistent effort.

Personal Growth and Attachment

Personal growth is the backbone of transitioning from anxious to secure attachment. It involves expanding your understanding of yourself beyond your attachment style. Engaging in activities that foster self-discovery and self-expression can be incredibly beneficial. This might include creative pursuits, physical activities, or even academic interests that challenge you and build your confidence. As you cultivate a richer, more rounded sense of self, your attachment system begins to recalibrate. You start to find security within yourself, which in turn reflects in your relationships. Secure attachment is not about never feeling anxious or always being confident—it's about managing your reactions in a way that fosters openness and intimacy rather than fear and uncertainty.

The Role of Therapy and Self-Help

While personal efforts at understanding and growth are crucial, the role of professional help cannot be overstated. Therapy offers a structured environment where you can explore your attachment issues with guidance from someone who can provide objective insight and evidence-based strategies. Therapists trained in attachment theory can help you identify your patterns, understand their origins, and develop new, healthier ways of relating to others. Alongside therapy, self-help resources like books, workshops, and online courses can supplement your growth. They offer flexibility and additional perspectives that can enrich your understanding and application of secure attachment principles.

Celebrating Small Wins

On this path, every step forward deserves recognition. Small wins might include recognizing when you're projecting past fears onto current relationships, expressing your needs assertively, or setting boundaries that protect your emotional well-being. Each of these achievements is a building block in the foundation of a secure attachment style. Celebrating these wins not only reinforces positive changes but also bolsters your motivation to continue this journey. It's essential to document these moments, perhaps in a journal or through conversations with supportive friends or a therapist. Reflecting on how far you've come can be a powerful reminder that change is possible and that you are capable of reshaping your attachment style for healthier and more fulfilling relationships.

Reflective Journaling Prompt

To deepen your engagement with the journey from anxious to secure attachment, consider this journaling prompt: Write about a recent relationship interaction in which you noticed old patterns of anxiety emerging. Describe the situation and your initial reaction. Then, reflect on how you might handle the same situation by applying a secure attachment approach. What would you say? How would you express your feelings and needs? This exercise can help you visualize and practice secure attachment behaviors, making them more accessible in your real-life interactions.

Cultivating Self-Love: Beyond the Buzzword

Self-love often finds itself entangled in misconceptions, portrayed either as a hallmark of selfishness or as a trendy buzzword on social media platforms. However, in the realm of anxious attachment, self-love takes on a profound and healing significance. It is not about narcissism or an inflated sense of self-importance, but rather about fostering a compassionate and accepting relationship with oneself. For those navigating the challenges of anxious attachment, self-love becomes a crucial pillar in reconstructing a sense of worth and stability that does not solely hinge on the perceptions or actions of others.

Cultivating self-love involves intentional practices that reinforce your intrinsic value and foster resilience against the tide of self-doubt that often accompanies anxious attachment. One effective practice is journaling, which provides a private space to confront and soothe the critical voices that can dominate your thoughts. This could involve writing letters to yourself from a perspective of kindness, detailing things you appreciate about yourself or achievements you are proud of. Each entry acts as a counterbalance to the often automatic self-criticism, gradually wiring your brain to recognize and celebrate your worth.

Moreover, establishing self-care routines plays a pivotal role in nurturing self-love. These routines should cater to both physical and emotional well-being—ranging from regular exercise, which enhances mood through the release of endorphins, to setting aside time for hobbies that bring you joy and peace. The key is consistency and personalization; your self-care routines should reflect what truly resonates with you, not what is popular or recommended by others. Whether it's reading, hiking, meditating, or painting, these activities should be engaged in regularly to reinforce the idea that your well-being is a priority worth investing in.

Mindfulness practices also significantly bolster self-love, especially for those with anxious attachment. Mindfulness encourages present-moment awareness and helps break the cycle of rumination and worry about past or future relationships. Through techniques like focused breathing, body scans, or mindful walking, you learn to observe your thoughts and feelings without judgment. This practice fosters an attitude of acceptance, allowing you to meet yourself where you are, with all your imperfections and strengths, which is the essence of self-love.

Transitioning to how self-love impacts relationships, it's transformative. By creating a loving and compassionate relationship with yourself, you diminish the reliance on external validation to feel appreciated or loved. This shift fundamentally changes how you interact in relationships. No longer driven by a fear of not being enough, you can engage with partners from a place of completeness and self-assurance. This secure footing allows for healthier dynamics in relationships where communication is open, needs are expressed constructively, and personal boundaries are respected. In essence, self-love equips you to participate in partnerships that are balanced and fulfilling, rather than those characterized by dependency and fear of abandonment.

In overcoming the self-criticism that often shadows those with anxious attachment, the strategy lies in actively changing the internal dialogue. Begin by identifying the harsh, critical statements that frequently populate your thoughts. Each identified thought can be challenged and reformulated into a statement that is supportive and true. For instance, change "I'm too needy, and no one can put up with me" to "I have a lot of love to give, and I am learning to express my needs healthily." This reframing is not about denying your feelings or self-deceiving but about viewing your attributes and actions through a lens of understanding and kindness. Over time, this practice reshapes your self-perception, enabling you to view yourself as worthy of love and capable of maintaining healthy relationships.

By integrating these practices into your daily life, self-love becomes more than a concept—it becomes a transformative force that enhances your relationship with yourself and with others. Through journaling, self-care, mindfulness, and reframing critical thoughts, you build a foundation of self-respect and appreciation that supports the development of secure, loving relationships. Remember, each step taken to cultivate self-love not only benefits you but also every relationship you are part of.

The Role of Forgiveness in Healing Attachment Wounds

Forgiveness, often viewed through a spiritual or moral lens, holds a pivotal role in psychological healing, particularly when mending the deep-seated wounds of anxious attachment. For someone grappling with this style of attachment, past hurts—be they inconsistencies in parental affection or betrayals in romantic relationships—can leave a lasting imprint, shaping how one perceives trust, love, and security. Forgiving oneself and others is not about excusing hurtful behaviors or forgetting the pain they caused; instead, it is about releasing the hold that these past experiences have on your present emotional life. This release is crucial for anyone seeking to move toward a more secure and fulfilling way of relating to others.

Self-forgiveness is an essential yet often overlooked aspect of this healing process. It involves addressing the harsh self-judgments that accompany mistakes or perceived shortcomings in your relationships. Perhaps you berate yourself for being "too needy" or "over-sensitive," which are judgments that stem from deeper fears of not being worthy of love unless you are without flaws. The practice of self-forgiveness allows you to accept that, like everyone, you are on a learning path—that each step, whether backward or forward, is part of growing into a more emotionally resilient individual. It helps soften the internal dialogue from one of criticism to one of encouragement, which is essential for internal security and self-compassion.

Forgiving others, particularly caregivers or past partners who might have contributed to the development of anxious attachment patterns is equally critical. This aspect of forgiveness might involve acknowledging the limitations or unresolved issues of parents who could not provide consistent emotional support. Understanding their human frailties can pave the way for releasing feelings of resentment or betrayal that may have been carried into adult relationships. It's essential to recognize that this form of forgiveness does not mean you condone what happened; it means you are choosing to liberate yourself from the emotional shackles of past experiences to reclaim your peace and emotional autonomy.

Navigating the journey of forgiveness is indeed a process—one that is often nonlinear and fraught with emotional complexities. It might begin with a conscious decision to forgive, followed by periods of doubt and resentment, before moving deeper into emotional release. This process may also require revisiting painful memories or discussing old wounds in therapy or through supportive conversations with trusted friends or mentors. Such discussions can provide new perspectives and insights that facilitate the forgiveness process, helping to frame past experiences in a way that fosters understanding and compassion.

The freedom that comes with letting go of the past is profound. It opens up emotional space for healthier relationships and a more secure attachment style. When you are no longer bound by the grievances of past relationships, you are more open to experiencing the present fully and joyfully. This newfound freedom supports the development of relationships based on mutual respect, affection, and genuine connection rather than fear and dependency. It allows for interactions that are not colored by the need for constant reassurance or fear of abandonment, which are hallmarks of anxious attachment. Thus, forgiveness is not just a gift you give to others but a crucial step in reclaiming your emotional well-being and paving the way for more secure and satisfying relationships.

Preparing for Setbacks: Resilience in the Healing Process

Setbacks are an inevitable part of any growth process, including the transition from anxious to secure attachment. It's important to understand that progress is not always linear and that experiencing a setback does not mean you have failed or are back to square one.

Instead, these moments are integral to the learning curve, offering rich insights that can fortify your journey towards secure attachment. Embracing setbacks with an open heart and without self-judgment allows you to navigate these challenges with greater ease and less distress. Think of them as signposts that provide you with an opportunity to pause, reflect, and recalibrate your path forward.

When you encounter a setback, such as falling back into old patterns of neediness or fear-driven behaviors in a relationship, the first step is to approach it with kindness and understanding. Self-compassion is crucial here. It's about acknowledging that you're doing your best and that growth inherently involves encountering obstacles. To build resilience in the face of setbacks, begin by maintaining a balanced perspective. This means recognizing the setback as a temporary and isolated event, not as a defining or permanent aspect of your journey. It's also helpful to recall past successes and how you've overcome challenges before, reinforcing your confidence in your ability to move forward.

Building resilience also involves practical strategies that equip you to handle setbacks more effectively. Developing a toolkit of emotional and relational skills can be invaluable. This might include techniques like deep breathing or mindfulness to calm anxiety when it spikes or communication skills to convey your feelings and needs more clearly in relationships. Another powerful tool is scenario planning, where you anticipate potential setbacks and outline strategies for handling them. For example, suppose you know that certain relationship milestones trigger your anxiety. In that case, you might plan to discuss these feelings with your partner beforehand or schedule a therapy session around these times.

Viewing setbacks as learning opportunities is another transformative approach. Each setback provides unique insights into your personal patterns, triggers, and needs. Reflecting on what led to the setback, how you handled it, and what you might do differently next time turns these experiences into lessons that contribute to your growth.

For instance, if you reacted to a partner's distancing behavior by becoming clingy or demanding, reflecting on this can help you understand your triggers for anxiety and develop more constructive responses. Engaging in this reflective process regularly not only helps you learn from setbacks but also integrates these lessons into your everyday life, enhancing your relational dynamics and emotional resilience.

A solid support system plays an invaluable role in managing setbacks. Surrounding yourself with understanding friends, family, or a support group who know your goals and struggles can provide encouragement and perspective when you're feeling down. These supporters can remind you of your progress when a setback seems overwhelming, offer a listening ear or advice, and celebrate with you when you overcome these hurdles. Their external perspectives can also help you see solutions or improvements that you might not recognize on your own. Moreover, if professional help has been part of your journey, leaning on your therapist or counselor during setbacks can provide professional insights and strategies, reinforcing your resilience and capacity to move forward.

Navigating setbacks with resilience transforms these seemingly discouraging moments into stepping stones towards a more secure attachment style. By anticipating and accepting setbacks, building resilience through practical and reflective practices, and relying on a supportive network, you equip yourself to handle challenges with grace and confidence. This proactive approach not only smooths your path but also deepens your understanding of yourself and enriches your relationships, laying a robust foundation for lasting emotional and relational stability.

Secure Attachment in Action: Success Stories

Imagine transforming the landscape of your emotional world, where the shadows of anxious attachment recede, replaced by the light of secure connections. This isn't just a hopeful scenario—it's a reality for many who have navigated the complexities of their attachment styles and emerged with a sense of security and fulfillment in their relationships. These stories are not only testimonials of personal triumph but also beacons of hope and practical guides for those still on their path to secure attachment.

Take, for instance, the story of Elena, a young professional who recognized her pattern of escalating minor disagreements into relationship crises, fearing that each conflict would lead to abandonment. Through a combination of therapy, dedicated self-work, and gradual exposure to relationship stressors, Elena learned to interpret conflicts as normal parts of a healthy relationship rather than threats to her security. Over time, her reactions became more measured, and her trust in the stability of her relationships deepened. Elena's journey highlights a common theme: the transformation from fear-driven reactions to trust-based responses is possible with consistent effort and the right support system.

Another inspiring example is Michael, who found himself repeatedly in the throes of jealousy and possessiveness, which he later understood as manifestations of his anxious attachment. By engaging in mindfulness practices and joining support groups where he shared experiences and strategies with others facing similar challenges, Michael gradually learned to manage his emotional triggers. His story underscores the powerful role of community and mindfulness in reshaping attachment patterns—tools that anyone can implement and benefit from, regardless of their personal history.

These narratives are as diverse as they are enlightening. While Elena found her solace through therapy and personal introspection, Michael leaned on community support and practical engagement with mindfulness. This diversity in paths to secure attachment illustrates a crucial point: there is no one-size-fits-all method. Each person's route to a secure attachment is unique and paved with personal insights, specific challenges, and individual triumphs. What remains common is the underlying resilience and the courage to confront and transform deeply ingrained patterns of thinking and behaving.

From these stories, several key lessons emerge that can serve as guideposts for your own journey. First, understanding the root of your attachment style is crucial—it provides the context needed to unpack why certain relationship dynamics trigger anxiety. Second, active engagement with therapeutic or healing practices is essential. Whether through formal therapy, self-help resources, or community support, these tools provide the mechanisms for change and growth. Third, patience cannot be underestimated. Just as these individuals did not reach secure attachment overnight, neither will you. The process is gradual, requiring persistence and dedication.

These stories do more than just inspire—they motivate. They serve as tangible proof that moving from anxious to secure attachment is not only possible but also rewarding. The emotional freedom gained, the depth of relationships possible, and the personal growth achieved are worth the effort. Let these stories remind you that change is within your grasp and that your efforts to understand and reshape your attachment style can lead to profoundly fulfilling relationships.

As this chapter closes, consider these narratives as both mirrors and maps. They reflect the struggles that might resonate with your experiences and chart the courses you might take toward healing and growth. As you turn the pages, let the stories of Elena, Michael, and others fill you with hope and determination. Secure attachment is not just a theoretical ideal; it is a practical, achievable state that enriches not just your relationships but your entire life. With each step forward, each strategy applied, and each small victory celebrated, you are paving your way toward a future where love is experienced with security and joy.

Conclusion

As we come to the end of this life-changing journey from feeling anxious to establishing secure attachments, it's essential to look back on the road we've traveled together. From the initial chapters where we delved into the depths of understanding anxious attachment and recognizing toxic patterns to engaging in profound self-work and healing, we've explored the terrain of our hearts and minds. We have acquired relationship skills and implemented practical strategies for a future filled with healthy attachments.

Central to this journey is the development of self-awareness and self-compassion. Remember, achieving a secure attachment begins with knowing yourself and treating yourself with kindness and patience. These are not just actions but a way of life that you continue to embrace.

We have also experienced the influence of mindfulness and the significance of establishing boundaries that promote well-being. These essential practices help manage relationship concerns, boost self-confidence, and foster loving bonds. Additionally, the value of honest communication, along with the courage to be vulnerable, cannot be emphasized enough. These components play a role in strengthening relationships and nurturing trust in any connection.

The pursuit of a secure attachment style is an ongoing process, so I urge you never to stop exploring new horizons, learning continuously, and evolving into the person you aspire to become.

The story doesn't end with reading this book. Surround yourself with a supportive group of friends, family, and experts who can help you navigate the complexities of an anxious attachment style and the relationship dynamics that come with it. Remember, you're not walking this path alone, and assistance is always within reach.

I aim to inspire hope and confidence in you, assuring you that you can attain secure attachment and healthier relationships by putting in the effort, being patient, and applying the strategies we've talked about. Take that step today not only for your own well-being but also for the health and happiness of your current or future relationships.

Recognize and feel proud of the bravery it takes to face and work through anxious attachment issues. Your experiences and challenges are valid; they highlight the courage needed to start on this journey towards healing and personal growth. Remember to consistently review your progress and celebrate your achievements. Set new objectives. If you ever find yourself needing support or dealing with challenges that seem overwhelming on your own, don't hesitate to seek out professional help or connect with support communities.

In conclusion, I want to leave you with a message: You possess the strength and capability to break free from the cycle of anxious attachment and create secure, loving relationships that you truly deserve.

Traveling through life can present obstacles. It also offers opportunities for personal development, exploration, and the happiness that comes from establishing meaningful relationships. You have the skills, the strength, and the value within you. Approach your experiences with a mind and a positive outlook.

Thank you for allowing me to be a part of your transformative journey. I wish for your future to be rich in love, empathy, and stability.

References

WebMD. (n.d.). Anxious attachment: How to know if you have it and what to do about it. WebMD. Retrieved from https://www.webmd.com/mental-health/what-is-anxious-attachment

(2017). Manifestation of trauma: The effect of early traumatic experiences on brain and behavior. National Center for Biotechnology Information. Retrieved from https://www.ncbi.nlm.nih.gov/pmc/articles/PMC5364177/

Harvard Medical School. (n.d.). Love and the brain. Harvard Medical School. Retrieved from https://hms.harvard.edu/news-events/publications-archive/brain/love-brain#:~:text=Released%20during%20sex%20and%20heightened,often%20associated%20with%20mate%20bonding

Mind Body Counseling Reno. (n.d.). How social media affects relationships in modern times. Retrieved from https://mindbodycounselingreno.com/blog/relationships/how-social-media-affects-relationships/

Bretherton, I. (1992). The origins of attachment theory: John Bowlby and Mary Ainsworth. Developmental Psychology, 28(5), 759-775. Retrieved from https://psycnet.apa.org/record/1993-01038-001

Schwartz, A. (n.d.). How relationships change your brain – Heal attachment. Dr. Arielle Schwartz. Retrieved from https://drarielleschwartz.com/how-relationships-change-brain-heal-attachment-dr-arielle-schwartz/

Pradeep, R. (2024, July 10). How oxytocin affects our relationships. Psychology Today. Retrieved from https://www.psychologytoday.com/us/blog/understanding-hypnosis/202402/how-oxytocin-affects-our-relationships

Ackerman, C. E. (2020, December 9). Mirror neurons and the neuroscience of empathy. Positive Psychology. Retrieved from https://positivepsychology.com/mirror-neurons/

Cleveland Clinic. (2021, October 13). Benefits of shadow work and how to start. Cleveland Clinic. Retrieved from https://health.clevelandclinic.org/shadow-work

MacWilliam, B. (2021, January 15). 5 art therapy exercises for healing anxious attachment style. Retrieved from https://brianamacwilliam.com/art-therapy-exercises-for-healing-anxious-attachment-style/

Cleveland Clinic. (2021, October 13). Benefits of shadow work and how to start. Cleveland Clinic. Retrieved from https://health.clevelandclinic.org/shadow-work

Psych Central. (2023, June 7). 4 at-home somatic therapy exercises for trauma recovery. Psych Central. Retrieved from https://psychcentral.com/lib/somatic-therapy-exercises-for-trauma

Chen, J. (2021, April 12). Mindfulness-based relationship enhancement benefits. Verywell Mind. Retrieved from https://www.verywellmind.com/understanding-mindfulness-based-relationship-enhancement-4685242

Calm. (2022, February 10). 7 tips on how to communicate your needs in a relationship. Calm Blog. Retrieved from https://www.calm.com/blog/how-to-communicate-your-needs-in-a-relationship

Mind. (n.d.). How can I improve my self-esteem? Mind. Retrieved from https://www.mind.org.uk/information-support/types-of-mental-health-problems/self-esteem/tips-to-improve-your-self-esteem/

Attachment Project. (n.d.). How to self-soothe anxious attachment triggers. Attachment Project. Retrieved from https://www.attachmentproject.com/blog/self-regulation-anxious-attachment-triggers/

Spiritual Primate. (2023, May 25). 50 shadow work prompts for attachment. Spiritual Primate. Retrieved from https://spiritualprimate.com/50-shadow-work-prompts-to-transform-your-relationship-with-attachment/

HelpGuide. (n.d.). Effective communication: Improving your interpersonal skills. HelpGuide. Retrieved from https://www.helpguide.org/articles/relationships-communication/effective-communication.htm

Ackerman, C. E. (2020, December 7). 23 resilience building activities & exercises for adults. Positive Psychology. Retrieved from https://positivepsychology.com/resilience-activities-exercises/

Therapist Aid. (n.d.). Creating secure attachment. Therapist Aid.

Retrieved from https://www.therapistaid.com/therapy-article/creating-secure-attachment

Verywell Mind. (2021, April 12). Why vulnerability in relationships is so important. Verywell Mind. Retrieved from https://www.verywellmind.com/why-vulnerability-in-relationships-is-so-important-5193728

Gottman Institute. (2021, February 10). 5 rituals to reconnect in your relationship. The Gottman Institute. Retrieved from https://www.gottman.com/blog/5-rituals-reconnect-relationship/

Flamme. (n.d.). Balancing independence and intimacy: Tips for maintaining individuality while having a strong bond. Flamme. Retrieved from https://www.flamme.app/balancing-independence-and-intimacy-tips-for-maintaining-individuality-while-having-a-strong-bond

U.S. News & World Report. (2023, June 15). Why is self-reflection important in relationships? U.S. News & World Report. Retrieved from https://health.usnews.com/health-care/for-better/articles/self-reflection-for-healthier-relationships

Van Der Spuy, R. (2024, July 10). How positive feedback loops empower relationships. LinkedIn. Retrieved from https://www.linkedin.com/pulse/how-positive-feedback-loops-empower-relationships-van-der-spuy

Hall, S. S. (2021, July 1). 5 things resilient couples do. Psychology Today. Retrieved from https://www.psychologytoday.com/ca/blog/brave-talk/202107/5-things-resilient-couples-do

Beverly Hills Psychology. (2023, May 20). Tips for successfully navigating major life transitions. Beverly Hills Psychology. Retrieved from https://www.psychologybeverlyhills.com/blog/tips-for-successfully-navigating-major-life-transitions

Collective World. (2023, May 30). The 3 healing benefits of shadow work. Collective World. Retrieved from https://collective.world/the-3-healing-benefits-of-shadow-work/

MacWilliam, B. (2021, January 10). How to self-soothe anxious attachment (a guide). Retrieved from https://brianamacwilliam.com/self-soothe-anxious-attachment/

Van Der Kolk, B. (2023, July 15). Nurturing secure attachment: Building healthy relationships. Psychology Today. Retrieved from https://www.psychologytoday.com/us/blog/the-angry-therapist/202307/nurturing-secure-attachment-building-healthy-relationships

Better Health Channel. (n.d.). Relationships and communication. Better Health Channel. Retrieved from https://www.betterhealth.vic.gov.au/health/healthyliving/relationships-and-communication#:~:text=be%20clear%20about%20what%20you,want'%20and%20'I%20feel

www.ingramcontent.com/pod-product-compliance
Lightning Source LLC
Chambersburg PA
CBHW030437010526
44118CB00011B/680